The WAY *of the*
STARS

The WAY *of the* STARS

JOURNEYS
ON THE CAMINO
DE SANTIAGO

Robert C. Sibley

UNIVERSITY OF VIRGINIA PRESS
CHARLOTTESVILLE & LONDON

University of Virginia Press
© 2012 by Robert C. Sibley
All rights reserved
Printed in the United States of America on acid-free paper

First published 2012

9 8 7 6 5 4 3 2 1

LIBRARY OF CONGRESS CATALOGING-IN-PUBLICATION DATA
Sibley, Robert C. (Robert Cameron), 1951–
    The way of the stars : journeys on the Camino de Santiago / Robert C. Sibley.
        p.   cm.
    Includes bibliographical references and index.
    ISBN 978-0-8139-3315-3 (cloth : alk. paper) — ISBN 978-0-8139-3316-0 (e-book)
    1. Sibley, Robert C. (Robert Cameron), 1951– —Travel—Camino de Santiago
de Compostela. 2. Spiritual biography—United States. 3. Camino de Santiago de
Compostela—Description and travel. I. Title.
    BL73.S55A3 2012
    263'.0424092—dc23
                                                                    2012008857

This book is dedicated to my son,
Daniel Cameron Kopala Sibley.

CONTENTS

ACKNOWLEDGMENTS

I want to thank the editors at the *Ottawa Citizen*, past and present—Gerry Nott, Neil Reynolds, Scott Anderson, Lynn McAuley, Christina Spender, Derek Shelly, Rob Warner, Julius Majerczyk, Kurt Johnson, and Sue Allen, in particular—who, in their respective capacities, contributed to this book, which first appeared in a shorter and different form as a series of articles in the *Citizen*. Gerry Nott, the current *Citizen* publisher and editor-in-chief, has been generous in giving me permission to turn that series into a book. I am likewise grateful to Postmedia Network (formerly Canwest Publications) for making my pilgrimage possible.

I am also grateful to friends and colleagues who have encouraged my pilgrimage efforts over the years. In particular, I want to thank Peter Emberley, Tom and Kay Darby, Waller and Jackie Newell, Tana Dineen and George Matheson, and Phil and Gail Ivanov. As always, my greatest gratitude is to my wife and fellow writer, Margret Kopala.

I would be remiss if I didn't acknowledge the University of Virginia Press humanities editor, Cathie Brettschneider. Her interest, support, and diligence in editing have made this a better book.

The WAY of the STARS

Santiago de Compostela

Ponferrada
Astorga
León
Burgos
Logroño
Pamplona
Jaca
Roncesvalles
St.-Jean-Pied-de-Port

PROLOGUE

Pilgrims are persons in motion—passing through territories not their own—seeking something we might call completion.

—RICHARD R. NIEBUHR,
"PILGRIMS AND PIONEERS"

I couldn't see my son. He was somewhere ahead of me on the mountain, but I'd lost sight of him as I labored up the muddy, leaf-slippery slope, following the trail as it wound through a copse of mist-shrouded oak and beech trees. We had started out together, Daniel and I, two hours earlier, leaving Saint-Jean-Pied-de-Port on the French side of the Pyrenees to take the Napoleon Route across the mountains to Roncesvalles on the Spanish side of the border. It was still dark, but the trek to Roncesvalles would take eight or nine hours and even longer if we ran into bad weather or inadvertently took the wrong trail.

Before we left Saint-Jean we had a quick, out-of-the-backpack breakfast of ham, cheese, and bread that we'd purchased the previous day. It had rained during the night, and we'd sat on a wet wooden bench beneath the dripping awning of the Brasserie Zuharpeta. The restaurant was dark and the windows shuttered. We'd made baguette sandwiches by the light of a street lamp across the road and eaten them in silence, looking out on the shiny wet asphalt. I'd felt oddly disoriented.

Eight years earlier, I had paused for a solitary predawn breakfast at the same shuttered café before embarking on my first pilgrimage along the Camino de Santiago de Compostela, the Way of St. James, one of the most famous pilgrim routes in the Christian world. Now I was here with my son, fulfilling a commitment I'd made to him when I was about to head off on that first trek. He was in high school then, and I'd promised that if he finished school and got a university degree, I would pay for both of us to walk the Camino after his graduation. He had kept his part of the bargain. I was about to keep mine. Yet I wasn't sure my heart was in it. I had fond memories of my previous journey, but I also knew how hard it could be.

As we ate I looked down Rue de Zuharpeta toward the town center and the long stone wall that enclosed the Parc des Remparts. On the far side of the park was the Hôtel des Remparts, also dark in the early hour. A gust of wind rippled the skin of rain on the road and rattled the awning, showering us with cold drops. I heard Daniel say, "Are we going to sit here forever?"

I smiled to myself. At twenty-four, he wanted to move. At fifty-seven, I wanted a nice warm bed. "Patience, my son. I was just remembering the last time I was here." Staring into the street I saw myself nearly a decade earlier trudging past, knapsack on my back, walking stick tapping the road, rain poncho flapping in the wind. As my younger self passed through my memory I asked him, "Why were you doing this? What were you thinking? Sure, you were excited, but weren't you a little scared, too, wondering why on earth anyone would go on a religious pilgrimage nowadays?"

"Come on, Dad," Daniel said. "You're always remembering something. Let's go."

My son was right. I was procrastinating, but not only because I wanted to delay confronting what I knew lay ahead. I was at an age when memories claimed more and more of my waking thoughts. I tended to savor those fragments of my life that memory had shored against my eventual oblivion. Still, the urgency of youth will have its way.

We cleared away our breakfast fixings, shouldered our packs, and followed the curve of Rue de Zuharpeta to Chemin de Saint-Jacques. I felt a rush of pleasure walking the empty streets in the cool damp darkness before dawn, moving in and out of one circle of street light after another, gazing at the darkened windows of the houses while imagining the lives inside, and hearing the echo of our hiking sticks as we tapped along the narrow road between rows of buildings. You're a pilgrim again, I told myself.

Yet as I tramped onward I kept thinking about my motives in wanting to make another pilgrimage. With the bounty of technology so readily available to make modern life comfortable and entertaining, there is something decidedly incongruous about undertaking a trek that entails considerable physical demands and long periods of solitude, facing the isolation of your own mind as you forego all the diversions our consumer society provides to keep us from thinking too much. Besides, ours is a hypersecular age that questions the point of a pilgrimage if there's nothing, or no one, to hear your prayers or to witness your performance. If you want to walk twenty-five or thirty kilometers a day and get all sweaty and sore, you can do that on a treadmill in your basement.

Of course in a less secular time like the Middle Ages, pilgrimages were common. Indeed, pilgrimage is a deep-seated trope of Western culture. Many of the great works of Western literature—Dante's *Divine Comedy* with its ascent to the stars, Chaucer's *Canterbury Tales* with its not-so-saintly pilgrims, John Bunyan's *The Pilgrim's Progress* with its everyman seeker—involve pilgrimage, journeys both inward and outward. But in an age when supposedly no Westerner of intelligence believes in a divine entity, why would you go on a pilgrimage? Yet millions of modern-day Westerners undertake pilgrimages every year. I'd read that more than six thousand religious sites in Western Europe attract between seventy and one hundred million people annually.[1] Why? Is such an apparent spiritual longing simply a reflection of the millennial zeitgeist, a desperate desire for transcendent significance in an age of anxiety? Perhaps the travel writer Pico Iyer got it right when he remarked that the contemporary notion of pilgrimage has a lot to do with people wanting to retrieve a sense of purpose in their lives, a sense of constancy, and perhaps a connection with something greater than themselves. But why in an age that worships comfort and convenience, speed and efficiency, would you spend weeks walking hundreds of kilometers? Why would you abandon the highways and bright lights to become, in Iyer's words, "a traveler into candlelight"?[2]

Good question, I thought, as I splashed through a mud puddle. On the surface, my reason for undertaking a second Camino pilgrimage was straightforward: I was fulfilling a promise to my son. But in my heart of hearts I had to acknowledge a deeper motive, a deeper longing. I wanted to replicate the extraordinary experiences of that first pilgrimage, experiences that had awakened me in middle age from my spiritual slumbers.

The first couple of hours after we left Saint-Jean certainly didn't promise anything out of the ordinary. We merely put one booted foot in front of the other as the trail grew steeper and a chill wind off the mountains blew in our faces. We hiked through the village of Huntto with its clutch of half a dozen houses. A pale strip of light broke through the overcast clouds on the eastern horizon. But it was still too dark to see much more than the vague shapes of farmhouses on either side of the road and silhouetted hedgerows cutting through the fields.

Daniel was already well ahead of me, but I lost sight of him only when we entered a dark wood. I told myself not to worry, though I knew how easy it was to get lost if you weren't paying attention. Trails crisscrossed the mountains, and a pilgrim who missed a trail marker or made a wrong turn could easily wander off into some obscure valley. I hurried to catch up.

My fatherly concerns were unnecessary. The trail eventually emerged from the copse of trees. Rounding a curve, I came out of the woods and saw my son ahead on the crest of a hill, waiting for me. Good boy, I thought, waiting to see if the old man can make it without blowing a heart valve. Admittedly, I was huffing and puffing by the time I joined him. As I leaned on my walking stick and waited for my breathing to return to normal, I looked toward the mountain peaks we would pass beneath as we climbed higher. I turned to look back down the trail behind and below us, gazing at the small, dice-like clusters of buildings and fields that seemed to rise up from the valley floor as the darkness slowly gave way to dawn. I could make out the glow of lights in Saint-Jean. As we looked over the valley we heard a burst of birdsong from the beech and oak trees nearby. Almost at the same time, the top of the sun broke over the crest of the mountains in the east, and the valley was suddenly flooded with light. It was like watching lava flow. The light rolled and spread across the land as the sun rose, pushing back the night to reveal a panoramic checkerboard of green fields, small villages, and patches of forest. I glanced at Daniel. The sight absorbed him, too.

It was moments like this, I realized, that had made my previous pilgrimage so meaningful. As the valley filled with light, the memory of that first Camino flooded my mind. I don't mean I suddenly recalled each and every event or detail. Rather, the sense of it as a whole, its meaningfulness, swept over me.

Now, nearly a decade later, while standing on a mountainside with my son, captivated by the glimmering green landscape, conscious of the pack on my back and the walking stick in my hand—the same one I had relied on previously—I felt the vault of memory open. And with the rush of memory came an emotional shift. I remembered the first time I'd seen this landscape and how it had occurred to me that if I'd come this way as a pilgrim three or four hundred years earlier, I would have confronted the same scene. With that awareness I journeyed across a psychic landscape. In a split second I felt myself restored to a premodern sensibility I'd encountered on my earlier pilgrimage. For a brief moment I dwelled simultaneously in two worlds, the modern and the medieval.

I glanced up at the still-dark western sky and saw a few stars between gaps in the cloud cover. A good omen, I thought, recalling how medieval astrologers believed the Milky Way hovered over the Camino and served as a guide to pilgrims. Once again I was a *peregrino*, a pilgrim on the starry way.

"Ultreya!" I said as I looked at the stars hanging above the mountain.

"What?" asked Daniel.

"Ultreya. It's Latin for 'Go forward, go beyond.' It was a pilgrim motto in the Middle Ages, something to encourage them."

"Sounds good to me," Daniel said.

And so onward and upward we walked—or, more accurately, climbed—in the light of a new day. I lost sight of Daniel again, but I didn't worry about him, or not too much. He made it to Roncesvalles long before I did. When I finally arrived, we walked a few kilometers further to the little town of Burguete, spending the night at the Hostal Burguete, where Ernest Hemingway stayed during fishing trips to Spain in the 1920s. In the dining room there's a piano inscribed with Hemingway's signature and the date "25/7/1923."

But I'm getting ahead of myself and, perhaps, unintentionally misdirecting readers. The pilgrimage with my son is not the story I'm going to tell here. That story is Daniel's, and maybe someday he'll tell it. I want to relate my first pilgrimage. That month-long walk across northern Spain has proved to be one of the most remarkable experiences in my life, a journey whose significance has reverberated in subtle ways long after I returned home. As I trudged up the mountain after my son, and in the days that followed, I found myself remembering places I'd seen, people I'd met, and things that had happened to me, including things inward. But what I mostly recalled was how that first trek had been as much a psychological—and, some would say, a spiritual—journey as a geographical one. I had journeyed along the Camino, but the Camino had also journeyed through me. That's the story I want to tell.

In this regard, I'm not offering a pilgrimage guidebook. There are numerous such books available as well as many websites devoted to the Camino.[3] Nor am I providing advice on what to wear, how to pack, or how to prepare for the walk, psychologically or physically. Again, there are plenty of books on these subjects. In any case, whatever advice I could give is implicit in the description of my experiences. Besides, researching the Camino, reading the accounts of other pilgrims, training for the walk, selecting backpacks and boots and other equipment all foster a pilgrimage mindset. It is this "pilgrim mind" that particularly interests me—what can happen psychologically and spiritually when you walk for a long time with a spiritual purpose. In other words, my story is a phenomenology of pilgrimage.

What did I learn or acquire on my inner journey? Well, as any storyteller knows, the telling is in the showing. Suffice it to say that once you've been on a pilgrimage, you're never quite the same.

1

PRAYER

In Roncesvalles I prayed for the first time since childhood. I wasn't very good at it. I felt self-conscious and embarrassed. The words and ritual gestures had grown rusty with disuse and, it must be said, disbelief. I made the effort nevertheless, imitating others as they crossed themselves and genuflected in front of the altar. In part, it was a matter of wanting to be polite and not look out of place. But I also recalled the Catholic apologist C. S. Lewis once saying that faith is an act of will as well as belief. You sometimes have to act as if you believe because faith, like morality, takes discipline and habituation.[1] Besides, I was in a Spanish church as a pilgrim, and it seemed to me that if I was to be a genuine pilgrim, then I needed to take part in the traditional practices of pilgrimage regardless of my skepticism. So, despite feeling awkward, I chose a pew, knelt on the stone floor, and spoke the long unsaid words: "Lord, hear my prayer."

I prayed for everyone I could think of: my son and my wife, my mother and my dead father, my brother and sisters, and my friends past and present. But then I started to imagine all the things that might go wrong on my walk, how I could get lost or sick or not find a place to sleep. And that reminded me of stories I'd read about pilgrims suffering broken legs, being knocked into ditches by passing cars, and even being attacked by dogs. I imagined a pack of dogs surrounding me in some remote village and wondered about other ways I might die until I realized I wasn't praying anymore.

I started over, praying it wouldn't rain too much and my legs would be strong and I wouldn't get too many blisters or suffer a heart attack. But then I started to think about whether someone or something actually heard my prayers, or whether I was just mumbling to myself, and if that was the case, then what was the point of praying? And that got me pondering my lack of faith and trying to remember when I had had any and why it had disappeared. But I'd had that debate with myself for years. I turned away from this train of thought as some lines from T. S. Eliot came to mind: "You are here to kneel / Where prayer has been valid."[2] That encouraged me to pray again, only I couldn't think of anything more to pray for. I remained kneeling, with my arms on the back of the pew in front of me, until my knees hurt too much and my leg muscles started to cramp. Finally, I sat back in the pew, trying to ignore my wet, muddy clothes and my fatigue and anxiety, and let my thoughts drift as I waited for the Mass to begin.

It was my first day as a pilgrim on the Camino de Santiago. During the next four to five weeks, I planned to walk nearly eight hundred kilometers—five hundred miles—across northern Spain to the Galician city of Santiago de Compostela. The route crosses the Pyrenees, the green valleys of Navarre and Rioja, the plains of Castile and León, and the lush alpine mountains of Galicia until eventually it reaches Santiago, where according to tradition the bones of St. James the Apostle are encased in a silver reliquary.

My walk would take me from the last week of March to the end of April. It would prove to be one of the hardest things I've ever done, physically at least. But it was also one of the most satisfying travel experiences of my life. I saw beautiful country, ate splendid meals, and became part of a living history. Best of all, I enjoyed periods of solitude that allowed me to recall places, people, and events I hadn't thought of for decades. And along the way there were a few psychic experiences that I've never forgotten.

Of course all of this was unknown to me as I tried to pray in Roncesvalles. This two-street hamlet, with its twelfth-century Augustinian monastery and a collegiate church, is the pilgrims' gateway into Spain.

My effort at prayer, inadequate though it might have been, was also a gesture of gratitude for my having made it through the first day.

An hour earlier I'd been stumbling along a snow-covered mountain path uncertain about where I was and fearful that I was suffering the early stages of hypothermia. I'd walked for nearly ten hours, enduring rain, snow, and wind as I trekked the twenty-six kilometers over the mountains between Saint-Jean-Pied-de-Port and Roncesvalles. By the time I reached the Spanish village in the early evening, I was wet, cold, exhausted, aching, and not a little shell-shocked. The sight of the monastery's slate-blue roof was a huge relief. It seemed a good idea to offer thanks to whatever powers might be.

The dull gong of a bell announcing Mass pulled me from my reverie. Four priests in white gowns and purple vestments entered the church to perform the Stations of the Cross. This first Mass in Roncesvalles was special. It certainly had much to do with my sense of relief at having made it through the day. But also I hadn't been in a church in a long time. I was entranced by the priests as they stood in a semicircle behind the altar chanting the liturgy, by the glow of the gold-plated goblets, and by the play of light on the Virgin of Roncesvalles, a thirteenth-century silver-clad wooden statue of Mary holding the infant Christ. Maybe I was lightheaded, but the Child's face seemed almost gleeful while the Virgin had a faraway look.

An old woman next to me in the pew tugged at my sleeve. The Mass had ended, and worshipers were approaching the altar. The woman gestured for me to do the same. At first I didn't understand. Then I realized the priests were offering a blessing to the pilgrims who'd arrived that day.

"¿Por los peregrinos?" I asked.

"Sí, sí, una bendición por los peregrinos," she replied.

"Gracias, señora."

I joined five others, three men and two women, at the altar. I hadn't seen them on the road. They looked neat and dry and cheerful. I thought they'd probably come by car or, to be charitable, were simply more efficient pilgrims than I was. The priest paused in front of each one to make the sign of the cross and offer a blessing. The ceremony goes back to the twelfth century when the monastery and its hospital took care of thousands of pilgrims. Even as late as the seventeenth century, the monks greeted twenty-five thousand pilgrims a year. They received food and shelter and, if sick, comfort. If the pilgrims were dying, they received the sacraments. According to my guidebook, an ossuary on the lower floor of the monastery chapel holds pilgrims' remains.

When my turn came I tried to put on a solemnly humble face worthy of a blessing. The priest ignored my bedraggled appearance, smiled, and blessed me the same way he did the neater pilgrims. Then he stepped back and led us in the Pilgrims' Blessing.

"May the Lord direct your steps with His approval and be your inseparable companion on the entire Camino."

"Amen."

"May the Virgin Mary grant you her maternal protection, defend you in all dangers of soul and body, and may you arrive safely at the end of your pilgrimage under her mantle."

"Amen."

With my soul supposedly in good hands I hobbled outside into the rain and returned to the Hostal Casa Sabina where I'd earlier taken a room. The needs of the body were paramount now. I wanted a hot shower, a wholesome meal, and a warm bed. In the room I exchanged my wet clothes for dryer ones, draping everything that was wet—socks, underwear, pants, shirt—on the radiator or on chairs that I dragged as close to the radiator as possible. As I soon learned, this was the standard routine for pilgrims. At the end of a day's walking you hang your clothes—inevitably wet from either rain or sweat—to dry overnight. It didn't always work. Many times my clothes were still damp in the morning. Not all pilgrim hostels, or *refugios*, have heat, or washers and dryers, but fortunately most of them have decent showers. My biggest concern, though, was my boots. Trying to keep them dry proved almost impossible.

I was famished after that first day's hike. I took my first meal in Spain in the white-walled dining room of the Casa Sabina, with its sword-and-shield ornaments and paintings of knights on horseback decorating the walls. I sat at a table by one of the windows that looked out on the road through town. I was the only customer and had the young waitress all to myself. I ordered the *menu del día:* a thick potato soup, baked trout in lemon with vegetables, and a bottle of *vino de la casa*. The soup arrived in a big silver tureen, which I emptied. The trout was so fresh that the flesh peeled away from the bones with a turn of the fork. The wine gradually took care of my lingering shivers.

As I ate and drank—the winsome waitress kept filling my glass; how could I say no?—I thought about the misery of the day's walk and wondered, with a kind of what-have-I-got-myself-into sense of foreboding, how I was going to walk the next 750 or so kilometers, and why. I didn't belong to any particular faith. Like many of my generation, I'd been brought up largely without religious devotion, and my schooling had been decidedly secular. If forced to answer the question of religious identity, I usually described myself as a reluctant agnostic. It was, no doubt, a glib response, but it tended to fend off more uncomfortable questions. So why was an agnostic, reluctant or otherwise, undertaking a pilgrimage?

I allowed the lovely waitress to fill my wine glass again as I pondered that question. The word "pilgrim" comes from the Latin *per agrum*, meaning "through the fields," and the adverb *peregre*, meaning "from abroad." The Romans used the word *peregrinus* in the same way we use *alien* or *stranger*, referring to a foreigner, one from abroad. To be a *peregrinus* was to leave the community and wander off across the cultivated fields into wild and foreign lands.[3] Did this ancient understanding of pilgrimage make any sense nowadays? There is precious little wilderness left in the world, and it's well-nigh impossible to escape the technology of global communication. We might feel estranged from our next-door neighbors, but the ubiquity of the Internet and social media means that none of us can be complete strangers even if we wanted to be. Besides, in an age such as ours—when belief in soul-saving relics, penitential suffering, and saintly intercession is regarded as superstitious ignorance, if not madness—it doesn't make a lot of sense to spend a month walking in rain and snow to reach a church containing a collection of bones that probably didn't belong to St. James anyway. And even if they did, so what? They were just a bunch of bones, long past their return-to-dust date.

As I drank my way through the bottle of wine, I knew I was being deliberately contrarian, waxing cynical as a salve to my waning enthusiasm. But I was bone-weary tired. My feet and legs ached, and truth be told, I was nervous about my own capacities. If each day's walking for the next month was going to be a repetition of this first day, well, I wasn't sure I'd be walking very far. To have such defeatist thoughts at the beginning of my journey was depressing. It seemed that not only was I physically unprepared for the rigors of pilgrimage, I wasn't psychologically prepared, either. But that notion merely made the question of why I was on a pilgrimage more imperative.

I gazed around the dining room at the stalwart knights and thought back to six months earlier when a philosopher friend had mentioned the Camino de Santiago in conversation. I had been moaning and groaning about the need to get away and wanting a respite from the breakneck pace of my journalistic life.

"Have you ever thought of a pilgrimage?" he asked.

I shook my head. "I'm not particularly religious."

"We're all religious," he said. "Anybody who asks themselves what it's all about, whether there's some meaning to their lives, is thinking religiously."

I didn't argue the point. "Why a pilgrimage?"

My friend then told me about the Camino. While its glory days had been in the Middle Ages, it had never completely disappeared. "Apparently it's undergoing a revival," he said. "A lot of people are walking it again. Why not you? Some time alone might do you good."

"Have you walked it?" I asked.

"Not my kind of thing, but it might suit you."

I didn't ask why he thought it might suit me, and we went on to other things. Still, he'd planted the seed of an idea. The seed began to sprout while I was doing research for a series of end-of-the-millennium essays I was to write for the newspaper where I work. I had read an article on Gothic cathedrals that mentioned the popularity of pilgrimages during the Middle Ages and how Santiago de Compostela had been one of the most popular pilgrimage destinations, after Rome and Jerusalem, for medieval Christians.

I then started dipping into books about pilgrimages.[4] One in particular—Edward Stanton's *Road of Stars to Santiago*—captured my imagination. Stanton, a professor of Spanish literature at the University of Kentucky, walked the Camino in 1989. At one point in his book he relates a mealtime conversation with a priest. The priest describes Stanton as "a person who bears the hardest of all crosses, the cross of disbelief." Such a cross, the priest says, reveals "what our Spanish philosopher Unamuno called the tragic sense of life. It recaptures the instant of the crucifixion when Christ asked God why He'd forsaken Him. The difference is that it was only an instant in Christ's earthly existence; from what you say it's almost your whole life." For whatever reason, the words struck home. I suddenly knew I needed to confront my own disbelief, my own tragic sensibility—that life is without ultimate or transcendent meaning—and perhaps the Camino was the place to do it. As Stanton puts it, quoting the priest, "The Road to Santiago is also a search."[5]

I was lucky, or at least I thought it was luck at the time. My editor at the *Ottawa Citizen*, Neil Reynolds, wanted proposals from staff writers for projects that would get us out of our comfortable office cocoons in pursuit of stories with reader appeal. I proposed walking the Camino de Santiago and writing a series of articles about the experience. To my surprise, the project was approved.

One thing I learned right away, as I began researching the Camino, was that I would be following in a long tradition. During the eleventh and twelfth centuries an estimated half-million people a year traveled the route, despite bandits, wolves, greedy innkeepers, dishonest guides and toll collectors, and the foulest of conditions. And that was when Europe's population was no more than seventy-five million. Just as Muslims today make the journey to Mecca at least once in their lives if they can, so medieval Christians undertook spiritual journeys, if not to Rome or Jerusalem, then to Canterbury, Walsingham, or Chartres, or—most arduous of all—to the shrine of St. James in Santiago. Even criminals made pilgrimages as penance for their crimes, with village authorities telling them not to come back without proof they'd actually done it.[6]

But then medieval Christians tended to regard earthly life itself as a kind of pilgrimage toward God. Possessed of that sensibility, they saw certain places and objects as bearers of spiritual power that would make you a better person and cleanse you of your sinfulness. Out of this belief was born an obsession with relics—the bones of Christian martyrs, a sliver of the True Cross, a piece of the shroud in which Christ's body had been buried—and with the places where those relics could be seen.[7]

We might mock this sensibility, but are we much different? We, too, betray a kind of spiritual longing in our passion for relics—crumbling pyramids, cities preserved beneath the deserts of the Middle East, propped-up artifacts such as the Parthenon in Athens or the monoliths at Stonehenge—although today we label our longing a search for history, not for God. For medieval pilgrims it was worth great hardship to reach the cathedral in Santiago and see the bones of St. James with their own eyes. Such sights put them in touch with the divine and reassured them of ultimate meaning and everlasting life. "In an age of religious sensitivity, pilgrimage fulfilled a real spiritual need," writes the religious scholar Jonathan Sumption. "By inflicting severe physical hardship on the pilgrim, it satisfied a desire for the remission of his sins and opened up to him the prospect of a second baptism."[8] And so millions of men and women from all across Europe traveled for months on rough and dangerous roads for a glimpse of eternity.

The Reformation, the Renaissance, and the Enlightenment weakened this devotion to pilgrimage. The reformist and later rationalist assaults of Luther, Erasmus, and Voltaire undermined the worship of relics. After the eighteenth century the popularity of the Camino dropped sharply, and by the mid-1800s the route was declared all but dead.[9] Over the next hundred years, and well into the twentieth century, much of the ancient route disappeared beneath asphalt and suburbs or became a cow path between remote villages. Pilgrim hostels and hospitals by the hundreds fell into disuse and were closed or abandoned.

Not any more. In the early 1980s, several pilgrims walking or biking on roads along the Camino died in collisions with vehicles. The public outcry prompted scholars to dust off old maps and pilgrim accounts with the goal of restoring as much of the original footpath as possible. Spain, as a new member of the European Union, encouraged the idea. Newly formed Friends of the Camino associations began to clear the paths and set up directional markers. New refugios provided beds, showers, and kitchens. In 1985, Santiago became a UNESCO World Heritage City. Two years later, the Council of Europe, the cultural arm of the European Union, adopted the Camino as a premier symbol of Europe's cultural heritage. Thus the Camino was revived.

Church authorities in Santiago maintain a register of pilgrims. In 1989, they recorded 5,760 pilgrims traveling on foot, by bicycle, and even on horseback. In 1991, there were 7,274. By 1998, the number of pilgrims was approaching 40,000 a year. In 2000, which Pope John Paul II declared to be the Year of the Pilgrim, church officials predicted between 200,000 and 250,000 pilgrims. A decade later, church officials count anywhere from 150,000 to 200,000 pilgrims each year.

Most pilgrims—70 to 80 percent—are Spanish. But there are thousands from other countries, including Britain, Switzerland, Germany, Denmark, and France, as well as Brazilians, Americans, Canadians, and even a few Japanese. As in the Middle Ages, they come from all walks of life. Pope John Paul II visited in 1982 and in 1989. King Juan Carlos of Spain was photographed on his walk along a stretch of the Camino in 1993. The actor Anthony Quinn walked some of the route in 1999. Most famously, perhaps, the actress Shirley MacLaine, as she explains in her book *The Camino*, felt the urge to undertake a pilgrimage in 1994.[10]

But what in our avowedly secular and scientific age motivates modern travelers to undertake such a medieval journey? Some of the books by other pilgrims that I'd read treated the Camino as little more than an exotic adventure or, at the most banal, as a long-distance drinking party. Others, however, saw the pilgrimage as a way to appropriate the spiritual sensibility of a bygone age. Many people nowadays, wrote Pico Iyer, want to follow "in the footsteps of the past," leaving home in an attempt to experience something from another age and to acquire the spirit that once animated millions to make such an arduous effort.[11]

Was I, too, indulging in "pilgrimage by proxy," to borrow Iyer's phrase?[12] I asked myself that question as I polished off the bottle of wine and signaled the waitress, who was getting prettier with every glass, to bring another. Medieval pilgrims thought wine was a necessary stimulant for appreciating the Camino.[13] I took that as good advice and thought that perhaps more wine would open the doors of understanding even wider.

I recalled one night at home a few months before I left on my pilgrimage. I'd been sitting in the living room and flipping through Umberto

Eco's book *Travels in Hyperreality* when I came across his essay "The Return to the Middle Ages." There he argues that modern Western culture is hungering for a return to its medieval roots: "we are dreaming the Middle Ages," as he puts it.[14] The statement reminded me of something I'd learned about the building of Gothic cathedrals: to the medieval mind, all the elements of a cathedral—its flying buttresses, ribbed vaulting, stained-glass windows, and sculptured facades—were, in the words of St. Thomas Aquinas, "ordered toward God."

Looking around the Casa Sabina dining room at the fierce-faced knights on the walls and remembering my living-room revelation, I had to admit that part of me envied the certainty of spirit that Aquinas possessed, along with his confidence that time and space were divinely ordered. But the best motive I could claim for myself was the desire to escape the rut of everyday life, and I let that be sufficient justification for my pilgrimage. Indeed, the idea of a solitary long-distance walk when most travel today is for the sake of diversion and entertainment appealed to me. Walking the Camino was different from, say, a holiday hike in the Scottish highlands or traipsing around the Adirondacks. There was something appealingly unmodern about traveling by foot in an age devoted to travel by the fastest means possible.

Still, I couldn't deny a spiritual purpose or, perhaps more accurately, an impulse toward spirituality with regard to my pilgrimage. It was more than an extreme holiday and even more than a project for my newspaper. It seemed to me that to walk the Camino with serious intent was to attempt to slough off the carapace of modernity, to recover—or to imagine—a self I had lost. Over the course of a millennium, millions of people had walked through the same villages, climbed the same hills, crossed the same rivers, and visited the same chapels, churches, and cathedrals to say the same prayers and to receive the same blessings. By joining that ghostly procession I, too, was walking back in time. And didn't I, like those medieval pilgrims, also hope at the deepest level for some thaumaturgic event, some miracle of insight and revelation bolting out of the sky, some voice roaring out of a burning bush alongside the trail, some answer to my prayers?

I took another swallow of wine as my mind skittered away from the God question. The idea of "finding" God, of undergoing some kind of road-to-Damascus conversion, was too far-fetched, too New Age, for my secularized psyche. The Pope and Mother Teresa could talk about spiritual awakening with understanding and sincerity. Maybe celebrities like Shirley MacLaine could claim communion with angels. But the idea that some spiritual epiphany awaited me—well, I told myself not to take the notion too seriously.

Yet as I stared into my half-empty wine glass, I had to admit that the image of myself as an ascetic mendicant appealed to a part of me that I generally hid behind curtains of insouciance and cynicism. I wanted to walk where millions of people confident in their faith had walked before. Maybe something of their faith would rub off on me. At the very least, I wanted to experience something other than the life of comfortable consumption and entertaining diversion. I remembered something my philosopher friend had said when, shortly after he'd planted the idea of a pilgrimage, I told him I was going to walk the Camino but was uncertain about my motives. Uncertainty was a good reason for going on a pilgrimage, he said. "Sometimes you have to act before you know the meaning of your actions. The knowing comes after the doing." He quoted a well-known line from Thomas Merton: "We do not see first and then act; we act, then see."

And so, a few months later, I sat in a hotel dining room in Roncesvalles, remembering my friend's words as I started a second bottle of wine and went back over the day's walk in my head, trying to understand why I was doing what I was doing.

Like many pilgrims, I started my walk in Saint-Jean-Pied-de-Port, where I'd arrived the previous afternoon on a two-coach electric train from Bayonne. It was a crisp and clear day in late March. The spring sun was warm on my head as I followed the cobblestone streets to the Accueil Saint-Jacques on Rue de la Citadelle. The *hospitalero* on duty, Michel Mallet, signed me in and issued my *credencial del peregrino*, my pilgrim passport. I would need to have it stamped wherever I stopped each day in order to validate my journey. Once I reached Santiago I was to show it to the church officials in the pilgrim office. They would register my name in the cathedral's records and issue the diploma-like *compostelana* as proof of my having successfully completed the pilgrimage.

According to Michel, a trim and tanned fifty-five-year-old, I was the thirty-seventh pilgrim to register that year with the Amis du Chemin de Saint-Jacques Pyrenees-Atlantiques. He told me how in recent years he'd seen more young retirees walking the Camino. "They have stopped working at maybe fifty-five or sixty, but they are still young and wondering what to do with the rest of their lives. They hear about the Camino and decide to walk." Motives vary with each person, he said, adding that, in fact, the motives often change along the way as the pilgrim experience induces a shift in psychology. "The walking changes you," he explained. "You start off interested in the cultural experience and you end with something spiritual."

Michel warned me that the trek from Saint-Jean to Roncesvalles would be the hardest part of the Camino. You have to climb from an elevation of 180 meters at Saint-Jean to more than 1,200 meters just before Roncesvalles. At this time of year rain and snow were constant threats. I wasn't thrilled at the description.

After showing me around the refugio and introducing me to Janine, the caretaker, Michel offered a final bit of advice: "The first week is the most difficult part of the Camino, mentally and physically. Take care of your feet." We shook hands, and he asked me to send him a postcard when—if, I thought to myself—I reached Santiago. "Buen Camino," he said.

I was the only pilgrim in the refugio. The bunkroom, with beds for thirty people, was cold but cheerful. Large crucifixes and posters of French landscapes decorated the stone walls. I laid out my sleeping bag and began rearranging my pack for the morning. I had three pairs of cotton pants, three cotton T-shirts, a sweatshirt, a regular shirt, a sweater, six pairs of socks including three pairs of thick hiking socks, three sets of underwear, a light jacket, and a pair of gaiters. In case of rain I had a calf-length poncho and an oilskin hat. I also had a small medical kit. Then there was my walking stick, a hefty knife, and a two-liter water bottle.

In addition to notepads, my Canon camera, and a dozen rolls of film, I also carried five books: Elías Valiña Sampedro's map book, *The Way of St. James: The Pilgrimage Route to Santiago de Compostela*; a pilgrimage guidebook published by the Confraternity of St. James in London; my research journal, which contained several months of notes; and two volumes of poetry—T. S. Eliot's *Four Quartets* and R. S. Thomas's *Collected Poems*. I had sealed in Ziploc bags everything that could get wet.

Finally, I had two plum-sized stones: a black one from my son's rock collection that I intended to add to a thousand-year-old cairn, the Cruz de Ferro, halfway along the Camino; and a white one I'd found on a beach near Halifax a month earlier that I planned to throw into the Atlantic Ocean at Finisterre, a small seaside town west of Santiago that many pilgrims visit after completing the official route. It was all too much weight, as I would soon discover.

I felt restless. I left the refugio and walked to the seventeenth-century citadel that overlooks the red-gabled roofs of Saint-Jean. The mountains in the distance seemed like a looming wall. Heavy gray-bellied clouds scraped the higher peaks, and the snowline descended halfway down the slopes. That's where I'd be heading in the morning. I walked back into the old town to buy some bread and cheese, a couple of oranges, and a couple of bottles of water. At a gift shop I spotted a display of scallop shells. The scallop shell—*la concha de venera*—is the universal symbol of a Camino pilgrim. Pilgrims wear them around their necks, pin them to their hats, or hang them from their packs. The tradition dates to the twelfth century when pilgrims who reached Santiago received the shell as a symbol of their status and of the completion of their journey. I hesitated to buy one, thinking it was something I should earn. But then I thought, why not? I could use it as a talisman to prod myself along.

It was dark by the time I returned to the refugio, and I found that I had a roommate: Gerard, a Belgian pilgrim. Janine introduced us in the kitchen, where Gerard was cooking his evening meal. I soon learned that the sixty-year-old retired army officer was a veteran pilgrim, having walked the Camino several times. He'd begun this current trek in February, walking from Brussels. His face and arms were as brown as old leather and his body stringy. He planned to take a day off to rest before tackling the Pyrenees. "I have walked for fifty-two days," he said between mouthfuls of potato-and-onion soup. "Rain or snow, it doesn't matter, you just keep walking. That's the pilgrim way."

Gerard showed me pictures of his seven children and ten grandchildren. I couldn't keep track of their names, but I noticed there was no picture of his wife. They separated many years ago, he explained. He told me about a long-time woman friend who was in a Brussels hospital awaiting a breast-cancer operation. "I'm walking for her. God wants me to do this. I pray for her as I walk. I think of nothing else. Prayer and walking, that is all."

I didn't know it at the time, but Gerard would become my ideal pilgrim. I admired the purity of his purpose, especially compared to my own inchoate motives. After we turned out the lights, I lay in my sleeping bag thinking about what he had said and trying to imagine myself walking for two months across Western Europe. Prayer and walking, prayer and walking; I fell asleep with the phrase in my head.

There are two ways through the mountains to Spain from Saint-Jean. The Valcarlos route mostly follows a twisting highway to Roncesvalles. The other—the Napoleon Route—is more scenic. It partly follows an old Roman road that Napoleon Bonaparte took to invade Spain, and on a clear day it offers spectacular views. Michel, however, had said that heavy snow in the mountains had recently made the route impassable. As it turned out, the Valcarlos route was bad enough.

Actually the road was fine; I was the one in bad shape. I had spent a month making half-hearted efforts to prepare myself physically for the Camino. I should have spent six months in rigorous training. I hadn't anticipated what walking every day for a month with a heavy pack on my back would require.

The first couple of hours weren't too bad. I left the refugio when it was still dark, stopping only to have a quick breakfast on the terrace of the Brasserie Zuharpeta on my way out of Saint-Jean. The two-lane road out of town cut through valley farms and climbed gradually to the village of Arnéguy on the French-Spanish border. I liked the countryside: mountain slopes covered with oak, chestnut, and pine; green farms and orchards; caramel-colored cows with clonking bells; flocks of sheep on the upland meadows; and high overhead, wide-winged vultures riding the thermals. Spring flowers—bluebells, violets, buttercups, and here and there the fragile yellow of cowslips—filled the roadside ditches.

It had rained the night before, and the smell of damp vegetation saturated the air. A cool breeze carried the occasional whiff of cow manure. Birds sang, joining the gurgling rush of the Nive d'Arnéguy that ran alongside the road. Except for the smoothness of the wet asphalt and the occasional swoosh of a passing car or truck, it was a scene out of time, a landscape that I imagined hadn't substantially changed since pilgrims began coming this way. I saw no one else as I walked, although at one point I spotted some orange peels on the edge of the road; somebody else, another pilgrim perhaps, had been here before me.

During the Middle Ages the biggest risk for pilgrims wasn't the weather but other people. Robbery, assault, and even murder were common. One of the worst terrors was crossing the mountain passes between Saint-Jean and Roncesvalles, where, as chroniclers of the times related, bandits often laid in wait for pilgrims. I didn't meet bandits. The greatest danger I encountered was the cars whose drivers seemed to delight in riding through puddles just as they passed me. The truckers were more considerate, moving into the middle of the road and waving as they roared past.

I reached Arnéguy after nearly two hours. Its small cluster of white buildings marked the border between France and Spain. I noticed that my legs ached a bit, but I decided to walk for another half-hour to Valcarlos, three kilometers up the road, before taking a break. Just past Arneguy, it started to rain, sometimes mixed with snow.

So far as I could see, Valcarlos was not a booming town. There were a couple of banks, a few shops, and a church with a life-size statue of Santiago Matamoros—Saint James the Moor-slayer, distinct from the other depiction of Santiago as a humble pilgrim. I found the Hotel Maitena with its polished wood bar and brass espresso machine that gurgled and spit as it gave off little clouds of steam. It was pleasant to sit at the bar facing the picture window and look out over the valley below the town. I was the only customer. An elderly woman brought me a café con leche and a plate of tapas. She smiled in recognition of my soggy condition.

"¿Es usted un peregrino?"

"Sí, señora."

"¿Mucha nieve?"

"Sí," I nodded gloomily, looking out the window at the clouds low on the mountain slopes. There was indeed much snow. I didn't like the idea of walking in it. But when I finished eating, and after a second café con leche, I shouldered my pack, donned the poncho and draped it over my pack, and with a final "gracias, señora" walked into the rain and the snow.

Halfway between Valcarlos and Roncesvalles, just before the highway makes a series of switchbacks as it climbs through the mountain pass, the pilgrim route turns off the road and follows a narrow path along the side of a forest-covered slope. The path supposedly cuts the distance to Roncesvalles by a few kilometers. I took it. Big mistake. I may have been only a couple dozen meters off the highway, but it might as well have been a couple of kilometers. Above me on my right, the densely treed slope ascended steeply. It would have been impossible to climb. On my left, the path fell precipitously to a narrow gulley far below. It wasn't hard to imagine myself going over the edge and landing with a couple of broken bones in some thicket, prey for any wolves that might still survive in the mountains of Spain.

A layer of wet leaves carpeted the path. With each step I sank into puddles of water that quickly made a mockery of the sales clerk's assurance that my new boots were absolutely waterproof. Work crews had tried to widen the path by clearing bush and saplings to the edges, but that only added to my difficulties. Instead of hauling the cut brush away, they'd left thigh-high stacks of branches and the occasional tree trunk lying across the path. I repeatedly clambered and clawed my way over piles of wet branches, hindered not only by a heavy pack on my back and a walking stick in my right hand but also by a calf-length poncho that tended to snag. It didn't help that a sharp wind turned the snow and rain into freezing pellets aimed, as it seemed, right at my face. And all this time I was climbing. What was supposed to be a shortcut turned into an endurance course.

I pressed on. The snow came harder and thicker, and I had trouble seeing where I was going. I pushed and pulled my way through thickets of brush until at one point my feet slipped on a wet tree trunk that lay across the path, and I lost my balance. The weight of my pack pulled me backward, and I landed flat on the path but with my legs hanging in the air over the edge. As I fell, the front of my poncho pulled over my face. I lay like an overturned turtle, with my legs kicking uselessly in the air, unable to see, half-suffocated and half-strangled by the poncho tangled beneath and around me. I yanked it off my face with one hand and grabbed at the soggy earth with the other to drag myself away from the edge, immensely grateful when my boots gained a purchase on the ground. I used my legs to lever myself back onto the path. I think the only thing that saved me from plummeting to the valley below was my poncho snagging on the branches.

Lying on the wet ground while snow and rain fell on my face, I waited for my heart to slow to a more moderate gallop, wondering for the first time whether I was in trouble. I struggled out of my poncho, which wasn't easy considering that I was lying on it with a knapsack on my back. Eventually, though, I unclipped all the buckles and straps, pulled my arms free, rolled on my side, ignoring the mud and soggy leaves, and hauled myself to my feet. I was shaking, whether from adrenaline or the beginning of hypothermia I didn't know. How far did I have to go? Was it my imagination or was it getting dark? What time was it? I looked at my watch. Mud covered the crystal. When I wiped it off I saw that it was nearly 4 p.m. Where was I? I had left Valcarlos about 1 p.m. Surely I didn't have much farther to go. I felt panic rising in my chest.

Then, oddly, I heard Gerard's voice from the previous night in the refugio: "All you have to do is walk. Just walk. Everything else will take care of itself." Hallucination or not, it seemed to help. The monster of panic retreated to its lair. I struggled to put on my mud-smeared pack and cinched it tight. I found my walking stick. I didn't bother pulling the poncho over myself—I was soaked and mud-splattered anyway— but wrapped it as best I could around my backpack in hopes of keeping the contents dry. I jammed my now wet and dripping hat on my head and plodded onward. The rain and snow still fell hard and steady, the occasional ice pellets sounding like a shower of lead buckshot on my poncho. My back and my legs ached, but I walked on, chanting to myself, "Rain or snow, you just keep walking. That's the pilgrim way."

In the old days, pilgrims sometimes died in these mountains during the winter, their gnawed bones found in the spring. I remembered reading one chronicler who, crossing the Pyrenees in the twelfth century, observed how thousands of pilgrims had died on the Camino, some lost in snowstorms while others, even more numerous, had been devoured by wolves. I tried to picture a wolf gnawing on my bones. Surely such things didn't happen in this day and age. Besides, there were no wolves left in Spain, right?

I checked my watch again; it was approaching 5 p.m. I'd been walking for nearly nine hours. I was definitely losing steam, and the light was fading. Luckily, I was hunched over, bending into the wind, my head lowered as I tried to keep the stinging sleet out of my face. Otherwise, I would have missed the orange peels. There at the edge of the path, their vivid color startling against the snow-covered ground, were four neatly quartered sections of orange peel, just like the ones I had seen earlier on the highway. The sight of them brought me to a halt. I stared at them in the pelting rain. Again I registered that somebody had been here before me. A fellow pilgrim had struggled over those damn piles of branches. Maybe he, too, fell on his ass. The image somehow cheered me. If the Orange-Peel Man had made it, so could I.

I started walking again, clambering over tree branches, stomping on soggy leaves, climbing another slope, and then another, and yet another. I stopped worrying about the time and how long I had to keep going. I ignored the sleet, keeping my head down and my eyes on the ground, not looking up to see how much farther I had to climb. I refused to look at my watch. I would get there when I got there.

I don't know how long it was before I stumbled into my second minor miracle of the day. I heard the tolling of a bell. At first I thought I was hearing things and beginning to hallucinate. Isn't that a sign of hypothermia? But I stood still for a moment and listened. Yes, despite the rain and the wind, I could hear the dull *bong-bong-bong* of a bell coming through the trees. For the first time in what seemed like hours, I looked up, and there above me, just beyond the crest of a slope in the trail ahead, I saw a cross. I staggered up the slope toward it. At the top I saw the slate roof of an *ermita*, or chapel. I had arrived at the Puerta de Ibañeta. At 1,087 meters, the Puerta de Ibañeta is the summit of the valley route between Saint-Jean and Roncesvalles. As I looked up at the cross, I felt a sense of elation replace my fatigue: I had made it. Well, not quite. I still had two kilometers to go. But the path was downhill and on lovely smooth asphalt. On the road, just below the chapel, I spotted a road marker saying "49 K." I had turned onto the path at "57 K." It had taken me nearly four hours to cover eight kilometers. Pathetic.

Twenty minutes later, I checked into the Hostal Casa Sabina. After dumping my pack in my room, I hustled to the monastery to get my pilgrim *credencial* stamped before the office closed and to attend the Pilgrims' Mass. I had to thank somebody for my deliverance—maybe the Orange-Peel Man.

Later, as I sat in the hotel dining room, well blessed, well fed, and if

I didn't stop with the wine, well on the way to a hangover the next day, I stared out the window into the drizzly night. I thought about how two days earlier I had been sitting in Le Fumaillon Brasserie on Place d'Italie in Paris, after a nostalgic tour of the area where I'd lived in the mid-1970s. The day before that I had dined at Capisano's in Bromley outside London, happy to be back in the English town where I'd also spent some of my younger years. And a day earlier I had been at home in Canada. Now I was in Spain.

As I drained the last drops of the second bottle, I knew my sense of disorientation was due to more than the wine or even my exhaustion. I felt the contradictory symptoms of the traveler who has moved too far too fast: anticipation and trepidation. There was a desire to be moving, to see what comes next, but at the same time I was hesitant and apprehensive. All those different times and places and memories shuffled around in my mind, looking for some sort of order and meaning.

My restlessness, and the need to clear my head, pushed me out into the rain for a final walk before bed. I didn't go far. There are only a half-dozen or so buildings in Roncesvalles. I walked along the highway as it curved westward toward Pamplona. At the edge of town, I saw the pilgrim path that runs for a short distance alongside the road between rows of poplars. At the entrance to the path was a wooden sign with the word *Ultreya* inscribed on it: "Go beyond." Beyond to what? I wondered.

Staring down the dark path, I thought of the advice I'd received from Laurie Dennett, the president of the Confraternity of St. James, a British organization that promotes the Camino, when I met her at the Confraternity office in London: "The Camino is a process of discovering the things you need and the things you don't need." What did I need? I returned to the hotel without an answer. The last thing I heard before I fell asleep was the monastery bell tolling the hour.

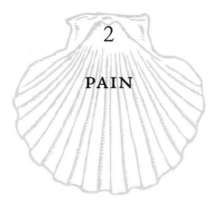

2

PAIN

The point of the pilgrimage is to improve yourself by enduring and overcoming difficulties.

—OLIVER STATLER,
JAPANESE PILGRIMAGE

The sun was shining when I left Roncesvalles in the morning. I interpreted that as a good sign, compensation for the misery of the previous day. Even better, the bar of the Hostal Casa Sabina opened at 7 a.m., allowing me a leisurely breakfast. My pretty waitress was nowhere to be seen, so I settled for a balding bartender to take an order for what became a favorite breakfast during my pilgrimage: a large café con leche and a couple of chocolate churros, sugared sticks of fried pastry for dipping into the coffee. I also imitated another patron by having a shot of anisette, the early-morning starter for Spanish laborers. Muscle lubricant, I figured. Not that my muscles really needed lubrication. To my surprise I felt pretty good. My legs were a bit stiff and my shoulders sore from the unfamiliar strain of the backpack, but the night's sleep had restored me. I even felt cheerful. There was none of the anxiety I'd felt the previous day. I actually looked forward to the day's walk.

By 8 a.m. I was on the pilgrim path, walking off the stiffness in my legs as I headed for the town of Zubiri, about halfway to Pamplona. It took all of five minutes to walk out of Roncesvalles. In the daylight I was able to appreciate the gray stone monastery complex—the Romanesque Chapel of Sancti Spiritus and the marvelous Gothic Church of la Real Colegiata—with its steep zinc and slate roof. I was now one of the millions of pilgrims who'd passed through this hamlet over the last millennium and received the blessings of its priests. I found the notion appealing.

At the edge of town I passed a weather-worn stone cross with a carved relief of the Virgin as I followed a gravel path—the pilgrim trail—into the forest. I paused for a moment to enjoy the warmth of the sun on my head and to breathe in the crisp morning air. I felt a surge of nervous excitement as I stared down the trail as far as my eyes could see, wondering where it might take me. It was a flat, easy-walking corridor with tall beech trees on either side. In summer the trees would provide much-needed shade. But now, in late March, with the green buds just starting to show, the sun fell through the bare branches, dappling the path with a shifting pattern of light and shade.

El Camino—literally, "the way" or "the road"—was marked every few hundred meters or so with painted yellow arrows or sometimes a slash of yellow paint on a tree trunk, a stone, or a fence post. These yellow markers—*flechas amarillas*—served as directional pointers to keep pilgrims from getting lost. In some areas along the Camino they were plentiful but in others less so. Over the next month I would become very fond of them, taking comfort in their presence. When I didn't see one for a while I grew anxious.

On this day the yellow arrows took me to Burguete. The white walls of the houses with their red-shuttered windows and green doors shone brightly in the morning sun. Occasionally, through an open door, I saw polished tile floors and a length of hallway leading to cool, dim interiors. Large terra-cotta urns filled with flowers or shrubs stood guard at the doorways. Some homes had armorial plaques on their exterior walls, evidence that people had lived there for centuries.

Walking past a shoulder-high hedge in front of a house on the eastern edge of town, I inhaled the sharp tang of fresh dill. The smell made me stop and peer over the hedge into a newly planted garden. I couldn't spot the dill, but the memory of my grandparents' house in my hometown of Hanna, Alberta, filled my mind. They'd had a small white house with green trim on the edge of town. A white picket fence encircled both the house and a large garden, one corner of which was thick with dill, which my grandmother used to flavor her soup.

The memory caught me by surprise. I hadn't thought of my maternal grandparents, Christian and Magdeline, for years. Immigrants from an area near the Black Sea that was once part of the Austro-Hungarian Empire, they had died when I was still a boy. Standing by the hedge, looking at the garden, I remembered the summer my mother, my younger brother and sister, and I had lived with them—I must have been nine or ten—while my father was away, working in Inuvik in the Northwest Territories. I'd spent my days pottering around my grandfather's tool shed, pungent with the acrid sweetness of the curled wood shavings that covered the dirt floor, or sitting in the big stuffed chairs on the enclosed porch reading *Huckleberry Finn*, *Tom Sawyer*, and *Kidnapped* as I half-listened to my mother and grandmother in the kitchen. Those books were among the half-dozen my father had given to me before he'd left for his job, telling me to take care of them because they'd been his boyhood reading, too. It felt strange to recall that Alberta summer—one of the best summers of my childhood—so vividly, and so unexpectedly, as I walked through a Spanish village. It was the first of what would be several such visitations I had from the past while on my pilgrimage.

The Camino led to Espinal—another of those picture-perfect villages that make the remnants of rural Spain feel like places out of time—and then into woodlands that climbed up and down until I reached the Alto de Mezquiriz summit and passed a stone pillar that urged prayers to Our Lady of Roncesvalles. I thought of the episode in Edward Stanton's book when he was hiking through this region in the late 1980s. He encountered a black-haired young shepherdess with her dress hiked up to her waist, bare legs and buttocks exposed, nonchalantly urinating on the ground. She'd smiled at him as he passed, well aware that he'd been watching.[1]

I enjoyed no such erotic vision, but there was a surprise for me nonetheless. On the ground beside the stone pillar were four quarter-sectioned orange peels. I remembered how the sight of such peels had pulled me out of my misery the previous day. Once more I had evidence of a fellow pilgrim ahead of me, and again I felt cheered. Not only could I count on the *flechas amarillas* to keep me on the straight and narrow, I also had the Orange-Peel Man to break trail for me. I stopped to rest. Sitting next to the pillar, I sipped a bottle of water, sliced my own orange, and wondered if I would someday meet him—somewhere on the Camino. I wanted to thank him for his inspiration.

Near midday I stopped for lunch at the Bar Juan, a clean and well-lighted café in Viscarret that doubled as a grocery store. I took a table at a window that looked out on the street.

"Por favor, señora. ¿Tiene usted alguna sopa?" I asked the middle-aged woman behind the bar in my clumsy Spanish.

The woman spoke so fast I wasn't sure if she was speaking Spanish or Basque.

"Perdón," I said. "No comprendo. Hablo español sólo un poco."

The woman smiled. "¿Peregrino?"

"Sí," I replied, acknowledging the obvious.

"¿Americano?" she asked.

That I understood. If I wasn't English, I must be American. "No, soy de Canadá."

"Ah, Canadá. Me gusta mucho Canadá," she added.

She kept talking, but I didn't understand what it was about Canada that she liked so much. North Americans are greatly outnumbered on the Camino compared to Europeans, so perhaps I was something of a rarity for her. In any case, I seemed to benefit from her fondness for my country. She went into the kitchen and returned with a large bowl of leek-and-onion soup and half a baguette slathered with butter. As I ate, I thought of the medieval legend about a French woman who had denied a hungry pilgrim's request for bread. He cursed her as he walked away: "May your bread turn to stone." When the woman returned to her kitchen and opened the oven, her loaf of bread had turned to stone. She chased after the pilgrim to beg forgiveness, but he'd disappeared. I suspect such stories were popular because they convinced pilgrims they were special and deserved better treatment.

This woman deserved only praise. Her soup was delicious—flavored, as it happened, with dill. It wasn't my grandmother's creamy borscht, but I ate two bowls anyway. The friendly indulgence of my hostess was something I would encounter throughout Spain, particularly in the countryside.

Not every pilgrim has regarded the Spanish, much less the Basques, so favorably. A twelfth-century French cleric from Poitiers, Aimery Picaud, the coauthor of the first and most famous Camino guidebook, the *Codex Calixtinus*, was scornful in his views of Spanish towns and the food and shelter he'd found. Naturally enough, being French, he described all things in France as *très élégant* and everything elsewhere as inferior. Indeed, so far as the monk was concerned, things went decidedly downhill as soon as he'd crossed the Pyrenees into Spain's Navarre region. Spain, Picaud wrote, was a land of dreadful food, poisoned rivers, and poisonous people. "For one sou and a half a man of Navarre will stab a Frenchman to death."[2] Picaud was equally scathing toward Basques. Their language was that of barking dogs. Their toll collectors were cruel, often beating pilgrims and robbing them of their clothes. They ate with their hands. They had sex with animals.[3]

Remembering Picaud's jaundiced views, I pulled my research journal from my pack and started flipping through it. As I ate my soup, I started thinking about the history of the Camino. The terrain where I walked that day had been the crucible of Europe. In the eighth century, the area around Roncesvalles was a killing ground where Christianity went sword to sword with armies of Islam intent on conquering the continent. The Moors had invaded Spain in 711 AD and soon possessed or controlled most of the Iberian peninsula, with the exception of a mountainous northern strip through which ran an ancient Roman trade route that would one day become the Camino de Santiago.

On Christmas Day, 800 AD, Charlemagne became the first Holy Roman Emperor, having united much of Europe that had been part of the Roman Empire. The effort had required a great deal of blood and treasure. Twelve years earlier, for instance, in one of his empire-building campaigns, Charlemagne had led his army across the Pyrenees into Spain in an ostensible bid to free Christians from Muslim rule. That, however, didn't stop his soldiers from attacking Christian towns. After Charlemagne's troops sacked the Basque town of Pamplona, the Basques took their revenge. On August 15, 778, in the forests near Roncesvalles, Basque partisans swooped down on the rear guard of Charlemagne's army, led by the emperor's nephew, Roland, as it returned to France. The slaughter spread westward as far as Viscarret and Linzoain, where, according to tradition, a badly wounded Roland used his final breath to sound his oliphant, his horn, to summon help, blowing so hard that the veins in his temples burst. Charlemagne, so the legend goes, heard the horn in the mountains and charged back to rescue his nephew. But he was too late. Roland was dead. A distraught Charlemagne sank to his knees and prayed. Moved by this supplication,

God stopped the late afternoon sun from setting to allow the emperor to pursue and slaughter the enemy and then to bury Roland in a copse of beech trees in Roncesvalles. Worshippers later built a chapel on the spot.[4]

Some three hundred years later the *Chanson de Roland*, the epic poem regarded as the cornerstone of French national literature, immortalized the battle at Roncesvalles. Some Camino scholars argue that the *Song of Roland* should be regarded as the founding document of the Christian West in the same way that Homer's *Iliad* provided the bedrock myths and symbols of ancient Greek civilization. With its emphasis on martial and religious virtues, including the ideal of noble self-sacrifice, the *Song of Roland* gave Christendom a much-needed moral self-image for uniting Europe against the Moorish threat.[5]

In the *Codex Calixtinus*, Picaud wrote a colorful account of the battle that cast Charlemagne as the first pilgrim to Santiago. According to Picaud, Charlemagne had a vision of a knight who identified himself as James, the apostle of Jesus, and who told the emperor to follow the Milky Way to Galicia to worship at James's tomb. But Charlemagne died in 814, four years after the discovery of the saint's grave, and there is no historical evidence that he ever visited Santiago.[6] Given the myths and legends that permeate much of the Camino's history, the shrine of Santiago might itself be a fraud. Biblical historians have generally agreed that James was beheaded by Herod Agrippa in 44 AD and was the first apostle to be martyred. His death is a fact. What followed, though, is the stuff of legend. According to tradition, James spent many years in Spain trying to convert the pagans. After his death his disciples, acting on messages in their dreams, took James's body along with his severed head and sailed in a stone boat to the Galician coast of northwest Spain. Skeptics have mocked the idea of a "stone boat," but boats carrying quarried stone around the Mediterranean were common at the time. It's possible the "stone boat" that carried James's body was a vessel loaded with marble or something like it. In any case, whatever the historical reality, legend has it that once the disciples landed, they used oxen to haul the apostle's sarcophagus inland, where they buried it in a field.

In 810 AD, a hermit named Pelayo saw the light of the stars shining on a particular place in the field. As he approached the spot, he heard angels singing. He told the local bishop, Theodomir, who ordered a hole dug in the illuminated spot. There they discovered a cave and found a sepulcher and papers attesting that it held the body of James the Apostle, brother of John the Beloved and son of Mary Salome, sister of Mary, the mother of Jesus. Theodomir told the Pope, who declared the site a pilgrimage destination. Soon enough worshipers built a church over the tomb, and a village grew up around it. Devout Christians, along with others not so devout, began traipsing the old Roman roads to the new city of Sant Iago.[7] The image of a field of stars—*compostela*, from the Latin, *campus stellae*—provided the pilgrimage route with one of its earliest titles: *el Camino de las Estrellas*, the Way of the Stars. The road to Santiago rapidly became one of the most popular pilgrimage routes in medieval Europe, and the city of Santiago, with its relic bones of St. James, the third holiest pilgrim destination after Jerusalem and Rome.

As I swabbed out my soup bowl with the last piece of baguette, I read in my journal how, for medieval Christians, certain places and certain objects possessed spiritual power.[8] These Christians believed that the presence of a relic bathed them in God's grace. Thus places where those relics were located became pilgrimage sites. We might dismiss this belief as unscientific, but if we want to understand the medieval devotion to pilgrimage, we need to recognize that medieval society was different from ours and more spiritually coherent, prompting pilgrimages in an effort to be closer to God. In other words, matters of the spirit were in some ways more important than material comfort.[9]

This devotion to St. James's bones had immense political consequences. The discovery of the saint's body happened at just the right time for Christendom. After Charlemagne's retreat, the Moors continued to dominate Spain, and Muslim armies constantly threatened the Christian north. But the pilgrimage's popularity enabled the Church to attract people, money, and arms to northern Spain, thus helping to establish a frontier from which Christian Europe could begin the *Reconquista* of Spain. In effect, the relics in the shrine at Santiago de Compostela stiffened Christian resolve against Islam.[10]

The political history of the saint's bones hasn't been without humor and, perhaps, some irony. A man known as St. Beatus, writing about fifty years before the discovery of the Santiago tomb, made one of the first attempts to associate James with Spain. According to scholars, St. Beatus used an old list of apostles and the places where they'd ostensibly tried to spread the faith as the source of his claim that James had been in Spain. The problem, as scholars later determined, was that the list had been copied from an even older list compiled by some anonymous scribe who had wrongly written that James's proselytizing territory was *Hispaniam*, or Spain, rather than *Hierosolyman*, or Jerusalem. In other words, the pilgrimage to Santiago de Compostela—widely regarded as having united Spain as a nation and given Christianity some breathing room against the Muslim onslaught—resulted from a misprint.[11]

Symbols, of course, can create reality. That was certainly the case with St. James. The earliest images and statues of the saint cast him as a humble pilgrim wearing a cloak and hat and holding a staff. This image changed in 845 at the Battle of Clavijo, where, according to legend, St. James appeared at the head of the Christian army as a giant on a white horse with a blood-red cross on his shield and with a huge sword that enabled him to kill sixty thousand Moors during the day's fighting. Thus was the legend of Santiago Matamoros—St. James the Moor-slayer—born, providing Spain with its patron saint and with a rallying cry for the *Reconquista*.[12] In churches and gift shops along the Camino, I often spotted statues big and small of Santiago Matamoros, a warrior on horseback, trampling the bodies of Moors.

The Way of St. James not only attracted the resources for restoring Spain to Christendom; it also gave Spain the wherewithal to branch out on its own post-*Reconquista* exploits after the last of the Moors departed the country in 1492. Under the banner of St. James, Spanish *conquistadores* and explorers marched through the New World. Some might argue that St. James was the patron saint of the West and the spirit behind its rise to world dominance.[13] Certainly, Santiago's reputation for intercession spread far and wide. William the Conqueror rode to the Battle of Hastings in 1066 on a charger given to him by a knight who'd made a pilgrimage to Santiago. And a twelfth-century *chanson* linked the Battle of Hastings to Roland's bravery at Roncesvalles.[14]

The Camino de Santiago held sway over the European imagination for more than eight hundred years, from the tenth century to the Enlightenment. Those who walked the Way of St. James were as varied as the pilgrims in the *Canterbury Tales*: princes and paupers, knights and knaves, courtly ladies and desperate prostitutes, pompous bishops and humble priests, saints and sinners. Chaucer's Wife of Bath bragged to her companions about the pleasures of traveling the pilgrimage road, but real-life pilgrims included St. Francis of Assisi, King Louis VII of France, and Catherine of Aragon, on her way to eventually marry Henry VIII of England. Her parents, Ferdinand and Isabella, the first monarchs of a united Spain, made the pilgrimage in 1496.

European culture is replete with references to the Camino de Santiago. I found notes in my journal referring to this cultural heritage. In *La Vita Nuova*, written a century before the *Canterbury Tales*, Dante defined a pilgrim as one "who travels to and from St. James at Compostela."[15] In *Hamlet*, Shakespeare's Ophelia alludes to the main symbols of the Santiago pilgrimage—the scallop shell and staff:

> How should I your true love know
>> From another one?—
> By his cockle hat and staff,
>> And his sandal shoon.[16]

And Sir Walter Raleigh began his poem "The Pilgrimage" with this depiction:

> Give me my scallop-shell of quiet,
>> My staff of faith to walk upon,
> My scrip of joy, immortal diet,
>> My bottle of salvation,
> My gown of glory, hope's true gage;
> And thus I'll take my pilgrimage.[17]

The image of the pilgrim wearing a long black cape and a broad-brimmed hat, bearing the scallop shell and with a staff in hand, also found its way into European painting. El Greco, Bosch, and Rubens all used the figure of the wayfaring pilgrim in their work. Velázquez painted the blood-red cross of the military order of the Knights of St. James on his own cloak in *Las Meninas*.[18]

All this has led some scholars to argue that the centuries-long mix of people from across the continent gave birth to a European self-consciousness and ultimately a sense of Western identity as pilgrims walked the Camino, sharing their ideas about the culture of their time.[19] Goethe said it best in his well-known phrase: "Santiago built Europe."

Mulling over the history and legends of the Camino as I finished my lunch in Viscarret with a glass of wine and another café con leche, I felt the first stirrings of my own sense of identity with the millions who had come this way before me. The medieval pilgrim had worn a long tunic and a broad-brimmed hat; I had my knee-length poncho and a wide-brimmed oilskin hat. My extendable Hillmaster walking stick substituted for the stout six-foot stave of long ago. And, like my medieval predecessor, I, too, possessed a scallop shell, which I had tied to the side of my backpack.

The pinkish inside surface of the shell was smooth and shiny and cool to the touch. Now flakes of dried mud marred the grooved outer surface of the shell, reminders of my fall the previous day. I rubbed the mud away with my thumb, wondering whether at some point in the next month of walking I would feel I'd earned the shell. Clothingwise, I had the trappings of a pilgrim; symbolwise, I wasn't so sure. But I was, at least, in good, if ghostly, company.

One of the things I would come to appreciate—and to hear others mention—was the historical resonance of the Camino: how in walking the route you felt a deepening awareness of history, a sense that you'd stumbled into a twilight zone where the past rubbed up against the present. Pilgrims make a kind of twofold journey as they walk the Camino—"a backward journey in time and a forward journey through space," as Walter Starkie put it.[20] It certainly seemed that way to me. There would be numerous moments along the Camino when I wasn't sure where I was in terms of time and space. I came to regard these moments as sojourns out of time, a brief psychic journey into the penumbra of history that encircles the pilgrimage like a ring around a harvest moon.

My first out-of-time moment came after lunch when I walked out of Viscarret and climbed through an oak and pine forest along a ridge over the Alto de Erro toward Zubiri. About a kilometer beyond the peak, I passed the ruins of the Venta del Caminante. Hundreds of years ago it had been a *posada del peregrino*, an inn where weary pilgrims could get a meal and a place to sleep. Now it was a crumbling ruin of collapsed stone and rotting timber, half sunk into the forest floor.

The climb left me hot and sweaty and tired. My legs ached, and I felt a hot spot on my right foot. I was an hour or so out of Zubiri, but I figured an afternoon siesta was in order. I dropped my pack and found a smooth patch of grass inside the ruins where I could nap out of sight. Lying next to some fallen timbers, looking up at the sky through the remains of the roof joists, I imagined being a medieval pilgrim and the relief I would have felt at finding this forest inn after a day worrying about bandits and wolves. After a while, though, the sound of the wind in the trees overhead proved soothingly hypnotic and I fell asleep.

I awoke maybe half an hour later, convinced I wasn't alone. I sensed a presence at the periphery of my vision, something just beyond my sight. I dismissed the idea as irrational, but I also knew I wanted to leave right away. In the late afternoon the crumbled walls had acquired deeper—impenetrable—shadows. I stood up, shivering in my sweat-damp clothes, belted myself into my pack, then clambered out of the ruin and back to the nearby trail. There was nothing there, I told myself, except perhaps my imagination.

I would have similar experiences in the weeks ahead. I refused to attribute them to encounters of a spiritual kind, as Shirley MacLaine claimed, but I couldn't deny that walking the Camino opened me to a preternatural awareness of the past: roads that had been built by the Romans, hump-backed bridges that priests and peasants had constructed half a millennium ago, village fountains where generations of travelers had quenched their thirst, and churches where stone floors had been worn into depressions by the knees of millions of pilgrims. I couldn't help but feel the presence of all those souls.

The walk into Zubiri only added to my sense of slipping into some psychic zone where past and present collide like tectonic plates. After the ruins, the trail descended steeply. It was less strenuous than climbing but also trickier to negotiate the sharp-edged bedrock that jutted up from the ground at haphazard angles. It dawned on me that I was seeing the results of millions of pilgrims passing this way. Their pounding feet and stabbing staves had worn down the forest floor, eventually reshaping even the bedrock. I recalled something I'd read about how each of us leaves thousands of molecules in our wake wherever we go, and that long after our passing, some of those molecules continue to mix with billions of molecules from others who have temporarily occupied that same space. I imagined myself wading through a sea of molecules left behind by long-departed pilgrims, absorbing the remnants of their passing and inhaling their lives until, by some strange alchemy, I turned into a real pilgrim.

I felt like a half-dead pilgrim by the time I reached Zubiri. I found the refugio in an old school and dropped my pack and myself on the bunk bed. My leg muscles thrummed at the punishment they'd taken, and my feet felt hot and sore, unaccustomed to the pounding. Some of the guidebooks I'd read advised wearing two pairs of socks—a thin pair of silk socks and a heavy pair of hiking socks—as a way to minimize the potential for blisters. I pulled off my boots and was relieved to find no blisters, although the balls of my feet were red and tender and the heels somewhat raw. I took a long and blissful shower to ease my aches and pains.

Before leaving home I'd prepared a cache of medical supplies that all wise pilgrims should carry, or so I'd read. It included medicaments for various intestinal maladies, sunscreen, liniment for sore muscles, Band-Aids, aspirin, iodine, and a needle and thread. I was a walking pharmacy. My most prized item, though, was a long roll of moleskin, an adhesive-backed, felt-like material I'd discovered in a chemist's shop in London. It was supposed to be effective for preventing blisters. I decided that in the morning I would be prudent and tape strips of moleskin across the balls of my feet.

After I'd showered and dressed again I left the refugio to find a grocery store where I could buy water, bread, cheese, and oranges. When I returned, I found I had company: a local woman who looked after the refugio and stamped the pilgrim *credencial,* and another pilgrim—a retired French businessman from Lille by the name of Charles Henri. He was the first pilgrim I'd met on the Camino, not counting Gerard. I was glad for the company. It was fine to walk alone during the day, but at night it was pleasant to be with others. After Charles settled in, we sat at a table outside the refugio, eating and talking. He explained that, at sixty-five, he had just retired and handed over his farm machinery business to his son. "I am walking for God and my family. That's what I think about when I walk—my family and my God." I wanted to ask what it was that he thought about God, but I was too embarrassed. It's hard to ask about God nowadays in such a secular world as ours.

When it grew dark we went inside and crawled into our sleeping bags. I fell asleep instantly. When I woke up, Charles was already gone. It was barely 7 a.m.

My third day, with twenty kilometers ahead from Zubiri to Pamplona, was the second worst day I would have on the Camino—the hike from Saint-Jean to Roncesvalles would always remain number one— although a couple of others would come close. For starters it rained most of the day, a steady, gloomy drizzle. Worse, though, I could barely move. When I awoke I found my leg muscles had seized up. It took considerable effort to stand when I swung my legs off the bunk. And even when I was able to stand, I was bent over like a question mark. I actually had to force myself to straighten my back to a more vertical position. But even more ominous were my swollen and tender feet. I applied a generous layer of moleskin to each foot, but I still felt twinges of pain as I shuffled along. Even my morning café con leche, enhanced by a couple of shots of anisette at a local bar, didn't put much spring in my step. Nevertheless, by 8 a.m. I was back on the Camino, putting Zubiri and the sour smell of its magnesium factory behind me.

Draped in my poncho, I trudged along in the rain for the next three hours, following a forest trail that ran along the side of thickly wooded hills above the Río Arga. It was slow going, because of both the soreness of my feet and the nature of the trail. The path was little more than a narrow gap between walls of oak and beech and pine. I could hear the river below, but I glimpsed it only occasionally through the trees. In the summer, with the trees in leaf, it would have been like walking in a green tunnel. But with the trees barely in bud, the rain fell unimpeded and turned the trail into a muddy soup. On flat stretches, I could step from rock to rock or walk on higher ground at the edge of the path. But when the ground sloped, I had to wade through a shallow, mud-thick rivulet. It was tricky keeping my footing on the slippery rocks. Every time my boot slid it was as if someone shoved a needle into my foot.

I emerged from the forest near the village of Uroz and crossed a short, hump-backed bridge over the river to a path that led to the highway. On the other side of the bridge I had to stop. I took off my pack, set it down, and then carefully lowered myself to the ground, leaning back against the bridge wall. I shivered as the chill of the stone penetrated my damp shirt. Slowly extending my legs, I hoped to ease the cramping in my thighs. I was grateful the rain had ceased, at least for a few moments. The sun even made a fitful appearance. If I hadn't been so sore and tired I might have appreciated the pleasant burbling of the river below me.

It was midday already, and I'd walked only twelve kilometers since leaving Zubiri. I was disappointed in my slow speed, or—more accurately—I was disappointed in myself for being in such poor condition. I knew I was supposed to go easy the first few days, let my body adjust to the new demands of long-distance walking. But even so, I hadn't expected to find walking twenty to thirty kilometers a day so hard or so painful. As a university student, I'd once worked on a geological survey crew in the Ross Mountains of the Yukon. I'd spent the better part of a summer walking up and down mountains every day. No problem, then. A quarter-century later, I wasn't pleased to find I was no longer so fit. Already the Camino was delivering a lesson: I needed to let go of my lingering attachments to a more youthful self-image.

Pride, it seemed, goeth before blisters. I calculated that I'd walked nearly sixty kilometers in the past two days. I was eight or so kilometers from Pamplona. Beyond that I had another 740 kilometers to Santiago. My mind skidded away from the idea. Dread at the prospect of failure blossomed in my imagination. I pictured myself having to go home with a note pinned to my shirt: "He couldn't cut it on the Camino." I'd read of other pilgrims forced to call it quits, victims of torn ligaments, swollen tendons, infected blisters, and even broken bones. Michel Mallet, the *hospitalero* in Saint-Jean, had told me the first week would be the most difficult, but was I going to fail where some Hollywood actress had succeeded? Maybe I needed angelic assistance, too.

I drifted into a half-doze and might have taken a long nap if the rain hadn't rudely forced me awake. It was time to go. Only I couldn't get up. Once again my leg muscles had frozen. I rolled onto my side and used my arms to push myself into a kneeling position. Then with the aid of my walking stick in one hand and with the other on the bridge wall, I hoisted myself upright. Stabs of pain ran down my legs. It was a struggle to lift my pack and thread my arms through the straps. A wave of dizziness staggered me. Low blood pressure? Heart attack? Stroke? I stood still for a few seconds, leaning against the bridge, waiting for my head to clear and my body to decide its future. When the dizziness subsided and the world looked more or less normal, I put myself in gear and lurched into motion. I moved like some rusted Tin Man, stumbling down the road through the slanting drizzle toward Pamplona, somewhere over the rainbow.

Two hours later I collapsed in a hotel room in Pamplona. That might sound as if I had stumbled along like a good stoic, but not so. It was pain all the way. I tried to walk on the sides of my feet, leaning on my walking stick, but that didn't do much good and only slowed me down even more. By the time I reached Villava, a suburb about two kilometers from my destination, I had no energy to follow the yellow arrows through a suburban maze into downtown Pamplona. I stopped at a hotel and asked a young woman behind the front desk if she would, "por favor," call a taxi. "Dios te bendiga, señorita," I said as I left. God bless you.

And so, in short order, I hobbled through the front door of the Hotel La Perla, where Hemingway had often stayed. They'd given him room 217, looking onto the Plaza del Castillo. They gave me room 113, looking over an alley. I didn't complain. I flopped on the bed—wet clothes, boots, and all. I had, I knew, cheated in taking a taxi. Authentic pilgrims don't use modern transport. Genuine pilgrims walk through the pain. Three days into my pilgrimage and I'd blown my pilgrim credentials. Frankly, just then I didn't give a damn.

I lay on my back for at least half an hour, not moving, and trying to work up the courage to face the damage. I'd quit smoking a few years earlier, but just then if someone had offered me a cigarette I would have gladly resumed the habit. I resisted the temptation to phone the front desk for a pack of Ducados and a bottle of Scotch. I thought about cigarettes until I couldn't bear my cowardice any longer. I lowered my legs over the edge of the bed and sat up. I propped my right foot on my left thigh, unlaced the boot, pulled it off, and dropped it with a thud on the carpet. I would clean up the mud later.

I didn't like what I saw. A large dark patch showed through the two pairs of socks on my right foot. When I pressed against the patch, my finger came away red. I peeled off the socks and cringed at the remains of a large blood blister that spanned the width of my foot just below the toes. The moleskin I'd applied earlier in the morning had bunched up behind my toes, and the blister had burst just below my big toe, causing the skin to shred and exposing the raw skin underneath. No wonder I'd been in pain. The whole ball of my foot was red, tender, and smeared with blood. There was also an inch-wide and two-inch-long blister looped around the back of my heel. I was grateful it hadn't burst.

I took off the other boot. My left foot was a little better. The thumb-length blister that looped beneath the ball of my foot was still intact. So was a nasty looking blister on the base of my fourth toe. I was grateful for small mercies.

It was obvious I'd made a mistake in buying my boots. I should have purchased them at least half a size larger than my normal shoe size. I hadn't thought my feet would swell so much from all the walking. A sense of failure washed over me. I simply wasn't prepared for this trek, physically or mentally. And now, looking at the bloody mess of my feet, I knew I wasn't going to walk for a while.

3

PATHS

Traveler, there is no path,
paths are made by walking.
—ANTONIO MACHADO,
FIELDS OF CASTILE

I sterilized the needle with my trusty Zippo lighter. I was careful to keep the flame away from my fingers, but it didn't occur to me that the needle would get too hot to hold. Only after I dropped it on the floor and was sucking my left thumb and forefinger did I remember the lesson from junior high science class about metal conducting heat. Clearly I hadn't been paying attention then, and I wasn't thinking too clearly now.

I picked up the needle and tried to sterilize it again, this time holding it with a pair of tweezers from my medical kit. I spent the next five minutes or so trying to thread it. Maybe I also should have paid attention in home economics class. I managed the procedure eventually and then held the threaded needle in my left hand and used my right to squeeze iodine from a dropper onto the thread. I let the drops run down the thread until I thought it was completely saturated, ignoring the excess that dripped on my bare legs and ran onto the bed where I sat. I should have put a towel down, but as I said, I wasn't thinking too clearly just then.

I propped my right ankle across my left knee, twisting my foot so the sole faced upward. In my research on the pilgrimage, I'd read about this technique for dealing with blisters, but there was no mention of what to expect once the needle was thrust under the skin of the blister and the iodine-soaked thread pulled through to the other side. There had been no warning that I'd shriek and flop about on the bed like a speared fish.[1]

When I finally stopped twitching and whimpering I sat up to finish the job, feeling like a wimp. I ran the needle back and forth across the width of the blister, trailing the thread of iodine, until I'd covered the length of it across my sole. I used my jackknife to cut the thread, leaving two inches hanging loose on each end of the blister. I did the same with the other blisters on that foot and then turned to my left foot. Now knowing what to expect, I shrieked no more. But I confess to some plaintive moaning and groaning through gritted teeth as I finished my pilgrim surgery. By the end of it I was sweating as though I'd run a marathon, and my feet looked like a red-stained scratching post.

Gently I pressed the blisters to squeeze out the water and any blood. I swabbed the entire area with iodine—more twitching and jerking—and covered the ghastly mess with antiseptic pads and wide strips of surgical tape. The idea was to leave the thread in the blisters to act as a poultice, wicking away the water and allowing the blisters to drain without exposing the even more tender skin beneath. The old skin eventually peels away, taking the threads with it.

I stretched out on the bed when the procedure was over, waiting for the sweat to dry and staring at the cracks in the ceiling. I felt sorry for myself. Looking at the debris—the bandage wrappings and the bed stained with iodine—it was obvious that all was not well with my feet. The only sensible thing to do was to take a couple of days off and let my feet heal as much as possible. So why did I feel like a failure? It was a pointless thing to feel. Who was I competing against? Who was judging me? Sure, I should have been better prepared and in better shape, but why was I so hard on myself?

As I lay on the bed, I flipped through my research journal until I found some advice I liked from a former pilgrim, who wrote that a pilgrim should know "when to be an ascetic and when to enjoy the good things of life."[2] Okay, I told myself, you're not going to be walking tomorrow or maybe even the next day. But you're in Pamplona, so enjoy it as best you can.

My best wasn't much just then. With my feet too sore for walking—I couldn't pull on my boots without some painful pushing and squeezing—I spent my first night in Pamplona waddling around my hotel room doing domestic chores. I cleaned my boots, swept up the dried mud, washed socks and underwear, and repacked my knapsack. I decided to leave some of my clothes behind to lighten the load. I thought of ripping out pages from my thick copy of R. S. Thomas's *Collected Poems*—it was a foolish amount of weight to carry—and keeping only those poems I most liked, but I couldn't bring myself to do it. I'd sooner toss out clothing than a book. I ordered the *menu del día* and a bottle of wine from room service and went to bed to read poetry and to get inebriated. I fell asleep to the sounds of laughter from the bars and restaurants in the Plaza del Castillo.

I was pleasantly surprised in the morning to find that I could squeeze into my boots without much protest. I could even hobble without jolts of pain so long as I moved slowly. I set out to shop and to explore the arcade that circles the plaza. My first stop was the Café Iruña, next to the hotel. Hemingway made the bar famous in his 1926 novel *The Sun Also Rises* as the watering hole of choice for his "lost generation" of characters. There was no way I was going to miss having a cold *cerveza* there while I was in town. I went inside and sat at a white marble-topped table beneath one of the big gold-framed mirrors that lined the gilded walls. I ordered café con leche and a *tortilla de patatas* and a few plates of tapas. It was a bit too early for a beer.

I gazed around the café while I waited for the food, wondering if it looked the same as in Hemingway's time, with its polished wood bar that stretched the length of the room, its golden pillars rising up to the high ceiling, and its wrought-iron chandeliers and globe lights. Did the waiters wear green jackets and black pants back then?

The tables were crowded with people lingering over demitasses of *café corto*, the thick, strong coffee that is the national morning starter in Spain. At a table in front of me four older men were playing a card game. Across the aisle, three young women, coats draped over the backs of their chairs, picked through tapas plates of olives and gherkins and shellfish. They were stylishly dressed. It was something I would notice everywhere I went: men and women, young and old, were well groomed and neatly dressed. I never saw a woman, young or old, in jeans or shorts, much less a halter-top. Men, too, unless they were working outdoors, were dressed in jackets and slacks and, more often than not, a tie. I wondered how long they could hold out against the North American fashion of adults dressing like children. In my baggy pants, sweat-stained T-shirt, and scuffed boots, I stuck out like a skid-row bum at a corporate board meeting. But then I was a pilgrim, or trying to be one.

As I sipped my coffee and munched on tapas, it occurred to me that I wasn't even properly dressed for the Camino. I'd basically outfitted myself with my old camping clothes, which consisted of cotton pants, T-shirts, and sweatshirts. Cotton, as I'd discovered, wasn't the best thing for long-distance hiking. Not only is it comparatively heavy, it also absorbs water easily and dries slowly. I needed something different.

I left the Café Iruña after breakfast to do some shopping. Just off the plaza on Calle de Chapitela I found Farmacia Gabas, where I restocked my medical kit with more moleskin, another roll of surgical tape, and several packages of Compeed, a marvelous skin-like adhesive pad that can be worn over a blister for days on end while the blister heals. I dropped everything off in my room and then returned to the street after asking the desk clerk at the hotel to recommend a sporting goods store. He directed me to El Corte Inglés, not far from the hotel, so I hobbled along Avenue de San Ignacio and down Calle Estella to the department store. I bought two pairs of fast-drying nylon pants with lots of pockets, a couple of quick-dry shirts with even more pockets, and a rain jacket to replace my flimsy poncho. Then I made my way back to the hotel with my new pilgrim outfit.

Once in the room, I checked my feet. The pad on my right foot was spotted with blood, but not much of it, and there were no signs of infection. When I applied more iodine I felt only a slight sting, which I took to be a good sign. I dressed the blister with another pad, wrapped my foot with surgical tape, and slapped a Compeed patch on my heel. The bandages on my left foot seemed fine. One more day, I thought, and then back on the road.

That night I dressed in my new pilgrim clothes and took myself out for a nice meal and a couple of long-promised *cervezas* at the Café Iruña. I pretended I was a character in Hemingway's novel and that I was dining with the wounded but stoical Jake Barnes and, of course, the lovely, Circe-like Lady Brett Ashley. By the fourth round I was imagining a witty conversation about lost faith, existential angst, and grace under pressure, none of which I could later remember.

I spent my second—and last—day in Pamplona playing tourist,

shuffling around the narrow streets beyond the Plaza del Castillo. I monitored my feet, mentally probing for signs of potential blisters. They were definitely better—though still sore depending on how I stepped—but I wondered whether they could take a long-distance pounding. Tense and restless, and still uncertain about leaving, I debated about waiting another day before returning to the Camino but decided that wouldn't be worthy of my newfound stoicism.

In the evening, I joined the locals—families with kids, young lovers, elderly couples, and gawky teenagers—as they strolled around the Plaza del Castillo beneath the still-leafless pollarded plane trees. I liked the way grandparents and teenagers walked arm in arm, the young ones often supporting their elders. I dawdled among the English-language books in Librería Gómez, a few doors down from Café Iruña, where I spotted a copy of Hemingway's short stories. I'd carried a white-covered Penguin edition with me for months during my first trip to Europe after university, reading it in cafés in Lisbon and Paris and on beaches in Morocco, until the only thing that kept it from disintegrating was copious applications of Scotch tape. I'd finally abandoned it in Israel, leaving it on the scarred headboard above the bunk in my room at Kibbutz Gonen where I'd worked for several months. The image of the book and that room, the details sharp as a photograph, nearly brought me to tears. I put the book back on the shelf, telling myself I didn't need the extra weight. But truth be told, I knew I was saying goodbye to a part of my youth.

I paid my respects to Hemingway—and to my youth—by toasting his memory with a bottle of cold Estrella Damm at the Restaurante la Dolce Vita, next to the bookstore. I walked off the beer with another circuit of the plaza and ended up at the Bar Asador for my evening meal. It had started to rain, so I sat inside at a table by the window and stared out at the empty plaza, watching as night fell and the street lamps came on, the wet asphalt glowing in the reflected light.

After a meal of *ajoarriero*—codfish cooked in olive oil, garlic, tomatoes, and eggs—I nursed the remains of a bottle of the local Navarre red wine and did some thinking. I'd read that 20 percent of Camino pilgrims who try to walk the entire eight hundred kilometers from Roncesvalles to Santiago de Compostela fail because of physical inability, lack of mental preparation, or disillusionment, which I thought might be the same thing as mental unpreparedness. It wasn't simply a matter of blistered feet and sore legs. It was also a matter of mind. I'd been mentally unprepared for the Camino, and if I didn't adjust psychologically, I might end up among that 20 percent. I remembered Gerard's advice: "Rain or snow, you just keep walking." Was that what I had to learn?

The more I thought about it, the more I realized I'd been fighting the road, trying to assert myself against the Camino. Every hill was an endurance test, something to master. I cursed the rain and railed against it. I kicked at rocks that threatened to turn my ankle. I bemoaned the mud that weighed down my boots. I loathed my clothes being wet. I knew that attitude wouldn't get me to Santiago. I couldn't beat the Camino; it was what it was, and it wasn't going to change. I had to change while walking it, not the other way around. I couldn't walk twenty or thirty kilometers every day for weeks on end, regardless of the rain, snow, or fatigue, if I was going to resent every step along the way. If I reached Santiago, it would be because I accepted the Camino on its own terms. I remembered a saying among pilgrims: "El camino es fe, sudor, y esperanza"; the Camino is faith, sweat, and hope. Okay, I thought, but it's also *aceptación*, acceptance. Or, as Hemingway might have put it, the Camino requires grace under pressure.

I remembered how years earlier I'd spent some time at a Buddhist retreat, trying to meditate, reading Zen poetry, and imagining life as a monk. Some three decades later, sitting in a bar in Pamplona, I recalled my long-ago fantasies about an ascetic life, and a phrase attributed to Zen Buddhism came to me: "When you sweep the floor, just sweep; when you eat, just eat; when you walk, just walk." Was that it? Was that what I had to do—just walk? Don't anticipate. Don't think about what is to come or what has gone before. Don't regret. Don't resent. Put one foot in front of the other, six hours a day, day in and day out, until you reach the end. Just walk.

I left Pamplona in the rain the next morning, sauntering along empty streets. The route was well marked with yellow arrows on lampposts, building walls, and even on the roads themselves. I appreciated the guidance. It was as if somebody was trying to help me on my way. I kept an even pace and made frequent mental scans of my body. Legs? Check.

Back? Check. Feet? Sore, but okay. Head? Who knows? Don't think. Just walk. And so I did.

Beyond Cizur Menor, a suburb of Pamplona, the Camino cut through farm fields until it began to climb gradually toward the Alto del Perdón. In the distance there was a long line of white windmills like giant sentinels along the ridge, their slender blades turning slowly. My guidebook explained that several dozen windmills supply power to Pamplona. I wondered what Don Quixote would make of them. At the top of a rise I saw other pilgrims ahead. The sight of them startled me. These were the first walking pilgrims I'd seen. I was tempted to catch up with them. But then I reminded myself: just walk. You will meet them if you meet them. Just walk.

At the top of the Alto del Perdón, I met the pilgrims I'd seen earlier. There were four of them—two men and two women—and they were eating lunch while resting beneath a set of billboard-size, cast-iron silhouettes of pilgrims on foot and horseback. The inscription on a plaque at the base of these figures reads "Dónde se cruza el camino del viento con el de las estrellas," or "Where the path of the wind crosses with that of the stars"—a double reference to the Camino de Santiago and the Milky Way. I dropped my pack and joined the group. We introduced ourselves as we ate: José-Luis, a tall, dark-haired young man from Brazil; Jean-Louis and Marie-Claude, a French couple; and Kerri Mooney, a blond-haired woman from Vancouver. They'd been walking together since leaving the refugio in Cizur Menor that morning.

José-Luis was the first to leave after lunch, followed by the French couple. Kerri and I walked together as we descended the Alto del Perdón, a major watershed on the Camino. Once I crossed it, I entered a different landscape. The poplars, oaks, and beech trees surrendered to a drier and flatter countryside of evergreen and chaparral. Looking west at the top of the pass, I saw the roofs and walls of villages I would pass through—Uterga, Muruzábal, and Obanos—on the way to Puente la Reina.

As we walked, Kerri shared that she'd quit her job as a tax lawyer in Vancouver and was considering an offer in Bermuda. "I want to do something to change my life," she said, explaining that walking the Camino gave her an opportunity to think things over. I would hear similar sentiments regularly during my pilgrimage. Several of the pilgrims I met, whether German, French, Austrian, Danish, or British, were professionals in their thirties to early fifties. They weren't necessarily dissatisfied with their lives, but invariably they wanted something more. While some expressed religious or spiritual reasons for undertaking the pilgrimage, most of them, it seemed, wanted an experience that would lift them out of their ordinary workaday lives, give them a glimpse of the extraordinary. The Camino, they thought, offered such an opportunity. Kerri, for example, said she'd heard about the Camino de Santiago years earlier when she was a student in London. The idea of walking it had stayed with her ever since, and when she quit her Vancouver job, she decided to give herself four weeks to walk as far as she could.

We reached Puente la Reina by mid-afternoon and stopped for the day. We each had our *credencial* stamped and then checked into a refugio run by the Padres Reparadores. Afterward we walked around the town and found a restaurant where we had dinner. Over our meal Kerri talked again about her job, the seemingly endless, and pointless, hours of work and how, now in her mid-thirties, she wanted something different. She startled me, though, when she said, "I knew I wouldn't die happy until I did this." I wondered if her motives ran deeper than she could, or would, admit.

The Camino encourages that kind of intimacy. I'd meet people and walk with them for a few hours or even for a few days. We'd talk about jobs and family and life back home. Sometimes we'd eat together in the evening. They'd leave the refugio before me the next morning, and I'd assume that was the last I'd ever see of them. But then we'd bump into each other again in some village down the road and have another meal together, commiserating about weather, blisters, and whatever else. In sharing the pain of walking and in swapping our abbreviated life stories, we developed a sense of *communitas*—loose and elastic, to be sure.[3] Sometimes, after we had exchanged snippets of our lives, I'd gain some modest insight into another pilgrim's motivation that would help me work out my own.

Kerri and I returned to the refugio after dinner to find it crowded with newly arrived pilgrims. Two major pilgrimage routes from France come together just before Puente la Reina. The town is most famous for a six-arch pilgrim bridge built over the Río Arga in the eleventh century at the command of Queen Urraca, who wanted to help the pilgrims on their journey. The bridge can get crowded during the summer, when many Spaniards walk the Camino. So, too, can the refugio. I'd read that desperate pilgrims sometimes get into fights over a place to sleep.

I never saw any fights, but it wasn't hard to imagine starting one. The refugio in Puente la Reina was a jail-like hole in the wall. The iron-and-spring bunk beds were crammed end-to-end along both sides of an unpainted, cement-walled room. The walls dripped moisture. For 500 pesetas—about $5—a night, I shouldn't have expected more. But it didn't help that the enforced proximity gave me too intimate an acquaintance with the foot odors, halitosis, and digestive workings of other pilgrims.

I checked my feet before I went to bed. Others, I noticed, were doing the same, including a gray-haired woman in a lower bunk across from me on the other side of the narrow room. Her feet looked as bad as mine. When I pulled the moleskin off my right foot, a swatch of skin came with it, along with the thread. The new skin looked pink and tender, but when I dripped iodine on it there was no pain. The blisters on my heels had also drained, leaving only loose remnants of skin that looked almost ready to peel away. The same was true of the blisters on my left foot. I was tempted to tear off the dead skin but restrained myself, slapping on more Compeed. My feet looked like they'd been stitched together by Dr. Frankenstein, what with the pinkish raw skin and the bits of black thread hanging loose, but my surgery had worked. The old blisters were healing, and no new ones were forming.

Although my feet seemed to be on the mend, my sleep fell short that night. Despite my fatigue from the day's walking, it took me a long time to drop off. Bedsprings creaked constantly. A pilgrim across the aisle snored like a Stuka bomber on a raid. Someone's malodorous underpants hung on the bed rail over my head. And never mind the farting. I had a fitful sleep at best, and when I awoke in the morning, Kerri Mooney had already left. So, too, had everyone else. I always seemed to be the last to leave.

I never saw Kerri again, but I acquired another companion that day—the gray-haired woman with the blisters: Anne Knowlan from Chilliwack, British Columbia. I caught up with her in the hills near the village of Cirauqui, about seven kilometers west of Puente la Reina. She was walking with three other women, strung out single-file along the muddy trail: Elizabeth from Denmark, Denise from Ireland, and Andrea Libia Lopos from Brazil. I guessed Anne to be in her fifties—fifty-eight, she later told me—while Elizabeth and Denise appeared to be in their thirties. Andrea was perhaps in her late twenties.

I would encounter Andrea over the next few weeks in various towns and villages on the way to Santiago. She was a voluptuous blond and possessed a kind of enthusiastic innocence, always greeting me, along with every other man, like a long-lost brother, with a big happy hug and a kiss on both cheeks. She reminded me of Charo, the hootchy-kootchy girl who had sometimes shown up on that 1970s show, *Love Boat*. I suspected she knew full well her effect on men. I affectionately nicknamed her the Brazilian Bombshell. Most times I saw her accompanied by one man or another doing his solicitous best to retain her attention. None of them seemed to last very long.

I walked with Andrea and the three other women to Villatuerta. Elizabeth and Denise decided to stop for the day, but Andrea, Anne, and I continued on to Estella through a landscape of vineyards, olive groves, and asparagus fields, their ridged expanses undulating across the land as far as the eye could see.

When the three of us reached Estella late in the afternoon, we sauntered through the streets with their small shops set back beneath *soportales*, or arcades, and wandered under the porticoes that encircled the squares, admiring the old churches and cloisters. French immigrants, who were repopulating land recovered from the Moors during the *Reconquista*, originally settled the town in 1090. Aimery Picaud had nothing but praise for the place. He wrote, "The bread is good, the wine excellent, meat and fish abundant." The town, he concluded, "overflows with all delicacies."[4] I couldn't quarrel with Picaud's judgment. Estella la Bella, Estella the Beautiful, was a lovely small town of green parks, narrow streets, and stone buildings that glowed in the evening sun. When we found the refugio on Calle de la Rúa, Anne and I checked in. All I wanted was a shower, a meal, and a bed. Andrea wanted something fancier and decided to find a hotel.

After the obligatory foot inspection, Anne and I explored the town, crossing the bridge over the Río Ega to the narrow streets of the old quarter where we found the Church of San Miguel. We climbed the wide steps to admire the sculptures. In the tympanum above the north door we saw the seated figure of Christ in His Glory, surrounded on each side by the Evangelists. We walked on until we stumbled into the wide expanse of the Plaza de los Fueros, with the Church of San Juan Bautista on one side and a line of arcaded buildings on the other. We crossed the square and sat at a table under the arcade of the Angela Pastelería. I ordered my café con leche. Anne had mineral water.

As we talked, I learned that Anne was a soon-to-retire librarian at a college in Chilliwack. Her husband had died of cancer a few years earlier, and her two daughters were grown. She was taking two months to walk the Camino and think about what she wanted to do with the rest of her life. After the Camino, she planned to visit the holy city of Benares in India, where according to Hindu custom the bodies of the dead are cremated on the banks of the Ganges. She was also thinking of starting a berry farm.

"I wanted to do something that was both physical and spiritual," she replied when I asked her why she'd decided on the Camino. She said she was Catholic and had heard about the Camino when she'd traveled through Europe in the 1960s. The idea had lodged in her memory, and now with retirement on the horizon, it seemed the right thing to do. "I hope it'll help me decide what to do next."

After our break we wandered through the streets until it was time for supper, when we returned to the plaza to study the menus in the windows of the restaurants. We picked the Bar Izarra for our evening meal. Inside, we met four other pilgrims, two of whom—Jean-Louis and Marie-Claude—I recognized. They invited us to join them. It was my first pilgrim "family" meal.

Our conversation inevitably focused on the Camino, its trials and tribulations, as well as its joys. Jean-Louis offered that, for him, the Camino was a gastronomic pilgrimage. His *credencial*, besides containing the regular refugio stamps, was thick with stamps from bars and restaurants. The best cooks in Spain, he declared, are the Basques, although the Gallegos in Galicia are a close second. At his suggestion, I dined on grilled tuna cooked with tomatoes, garlic, aubergine, and spices. I eased the meal along with a bottle of the light green sparkling wine called *txakoli*. There's a saying in Spanish, "A mala cama, colchón de vino," which roughly translates as, "When the bed is bad, there's nothing like a mattress of wine."⁵ So it seemed that night. I returned to the refugio feeling a pleasant glow and fell asleep immediately.

Although it would have undoubtedly been interesting to walk with Andrea, Anne became my first Camino companion, which was probably for the best. I enjoyed Anne's company for the next two days. After Estella, we followed the Camino through Azqueta, Villamayor de Monjardín, and Urbiola to Los Arcos, where we found the refugio in what had once been a school. It was a pleasant walk, although we got lost once and had to backtrack for an hour. By day's end, we were weary and footsore. My feet were holding up, although I noticed the occasional twinge in my right leg. That evening we went to a Pilgrims' Mass at the Church of Santa María with its massive Gothic cloister and High Altar covered in gold leaf. Unlike in Roncesvalles, I felt no self-conscious embarrassment in following the rituals, and when the young priest called the pilgrims to the altar after the Mass, I stood with a dozen others as he intoned the blessing.

"Lord, be for us a companion on the journey, the guide at the intersections, the strengthening during fatigue, the fortress in danger, the resource on our itinerary, the shadow in the heat, the light in the darkness, the consolation during dejection, and the power in our intention, so that under Your guidance, safely and unhurt, we may reach the end of our journey and, strengthened with gratitude and power, secure and filled with happiness, return to our home, in the name of Jesus Christ Our Lord."⁶

"Amen," I said along with Anne and the others.

The next day, the weather was utterly foul. Anne and I would have been grateful for divine intervention. Rain and wind lashed us all the way to the hilltop village of Sansol and on to Torres del Río at the bottom of the valley of the Río Linares. Our savior was Jordi Edo Julia, a rail-thin twenty-five-year-old from Barcelona. He was between jobs and thought walking the Camino would make a good holiday. There were a couple of times when if it hadn't been for Jordi, Anne and I might have gotten lost again and wandered off into the hills.

We staggered into the gloomy village of Torres del Río in the pouring rain at about 11 a.m. I was desperate for a hot coffee and some shelter from the rain. But nothing was open. That's when Jordi demonstrated his value. He walked up to a shuttered door and banged on it with his fist. When a middle-aged woman answered, Jordi started yammering in Spanish and gestured at Anne and me, dripping, bedraggled, and shivering. The door swung open, and we were invited into my idea of heaven. Jordi had found a bar—I hadn't spotted a sign or anything indicating that's what it was—and a patroness willing to heat some soup and make a couple of ham *bocadillos*.

It was a lovely establishment for such an unlovely town. The walls and ceiling were made of rough stone intersected by dark beams. A polished bar of blond wood stretched along one wall. Tables, scarred by cigarette burns, lined the wall opposite the bar. A fire roared in the hearth. I stripped off my rain jacket and hat and asked for a snifter of the Basque sloe brandy known as *pacharan*. I knocked it back and ordered another. Seated by the fire, I was soon glowing, inside and out.

We stayed long enough to eat and get warm. Unfortunately, when we met a couple of Spaniards, Jordi abandoned us for them. *Los Norte Americanos* were just too damn slow, I guess. Anne and I had walked about seven kilometers from Los Arcos; we had another nineteen kilometers to Logroño. It was a miserable hike. The trail was a quagmire because of the rain. Our boots collected big dollops of mud, and we stopped repeatedly to scrape them off. Walking was strenuous, almost hazardous, particularly when going uphill; the trail seemed to slide out from beneath our feet. Yet we both kept walking, not that there was any alternative. By the time we reached Viana around 4 p.m. we were exhausted. It had taken three hours to cover nine kilometers. Logroño was still ten kilometers away.

No way, I thought. Anne agreed. Surely this close to Logroño there would be regular bus service. We stumbled along the cobbled streets, asking "¿Dónde está la parada de autobús?" Eventually some helpful locals directed us to the nearest bus stop. The bus would be along in an hour. Lucky for us, there was a bar across the street where we could wait out of the rain. We took a table, stripped off our dripping packs and jackets, and ordered glasses of *vino tinto*.

My guidebook told me that Cesare Borgia had died in Viana, and his tomb lay under the street in front of the sixteenth-century Church of Santa María. At another time I might have paid my respects to the much-maligned Renaissance prince whom Niccolò Machiavelli had praised "as an example to be imitated by all who, by fortune and with the arms of others, have risen to power."[7] But it was not that day. I looked forward to a nice warm bus ride.

Anne looked at me and laughed. "Look at yourself in the mirror," she said, gesturing at the large mirror on the wall across the aisle from our table. I swiveled around in my chair. I looked like the proverbial drowned rat: hair plastered to my head, shirt and pants wet—from sweat or from rain it made no difference—and my gaiters caked to my knees in a layer of mud. I'd obviously lost weight. My face was wind-burned and my cheeks sunken, as though the elements were working to expose the bone beneath the skin. My eyes possessed a kind of glassy brightness. I thought I looked somewhat crazy, but maybe it was just exhaustion.

I may have developed a modest pilgrim look, but at that moment I was happy to sully the purity of my pilgrimage with a bus ride. One of the perennial debates among Camino pilgrims is who is or isn't a proper pilgrim. Some are embarrassed to admit that on occasion they've hitch-hiked or taken a bus or taxi. According to the purists, this indicates a lack of commitment and stamina, an unwillingness to endure the rigors of the Camino, a surrender to the culture of comfort, a forfeiture of the project to recover the spiritual values of the pilgrimage as laid down by medieval pilgrims. To this dogmatic notion of purity, I responded "pfffft!"

Nancy Frey, an American anthropologist who has studied the Camino and its pilgrims, has referred to this dogma as the "cult of authenticity."[8] Purists, she's written, believe that real pilgrims always travel on foot, possess a serious and even austerely ascetic attitude—no pleasures of the table, for example—and walk for at least a month. Authentic pilgrims, according to this view, are religiously or spiritually motivated, stop at every church they can to pray, stay only in refugios, and always follow the yellow arrows. By this standard, I was a failure as a pilgrim. I liked the food, the wine, and the occasional hotel bed. I mentioned this to Anne, saying that if we were real pilgrims, we'd be out there in the rain. She gave me a sour look. "Nonsense. I'm not here to prove anything to anybody." She paused. "Why would anybody else care, anyway? What's it to them? I'm staying right here until the bus shows up." I admired her good sense. It catered to my weaknesses. Besides, I was into my third glass of wine.

After a pleasant bus ride, Anne and I stood outside the bus station in Logroño shortly after 6 p.m., waiting for a taxi to take us to the Residencia La Numantina on Calle Sagasta. Half an hour later I lowered myself into a bathtub of water as hot as I could tolerate, sighing as the pains of the day leached away. Leaning back in the tub, I basked in my defiance of the pilgrim purists.

Anne and I had agreed to meet for dinner. So after my bath and with some time to spare, I went sightseeing. Logroño possessed the characteristics of many of Spain's old cities—rings of modern urban sprawl, with its attendant ugliness and lousy architecture, surrounding a gem of an ancient town. It was the same in Burgos, León, Astorga, and even Santiago, as I discovered. Flaking high-rise apartments, grimy factories, and boxy buildings enclosed a core, or *pueblo*, of cobblestone streets, lovely fountains, wide plazas, green parks lined with plane trees, and churches dating to the Middle Ages. Just before the iron bridge that spans the Río Ebro, I found the Gothic Church of Santiago with its massive equestrian sculpture of Santiago Matamoros above the main door. Then retracing my steps, I returned to the Plaza del Mercado near the hotel and sat on a bench to admire the looming bulk of the Cathedral of Santa María la Redonda until it was time to have dinner.

I found Anne at a table by a window in the Café del Mercado, a bright and cheerful restaurant across the plaza from the cathedral. As we ate I asked her whether she was serious about going to India. She told me the story of an Indian fakir she'd read about. This holy man spent his whole adult life in a deep pit in the ground, surviving on whatever food or clothing others threw to him. "Everybody felt sorry for him and asked him why he was wasting his life. You know what he said?" I shook my head. "He said he felt sorry for the rest of us because we had to spend all our time worrying about food and clothing and shelter."

"You want that kind of ascetic life?" I asked.

"No, nothing like that. But I do want to change my life. I think the Camino can do that, if you let it."

We had talked for a while longer when Anne told me she had decided to take a break from the Camino. Her feet were in bad shape after the last two days. I sympathized, but I was disappointed. I would miss her company. Anne then said she was tired and wanted to return to the hotel, so we hugged each other goodbye on the sidewalk outside the restaurant.

"I enjoyed walking with you," I said. "Take care of yourself."

"I enjoyed walking with you, too," she said. She paused. "The Camino can change you, you know. But you have to let it."

I didn't say anything in reply. We hugged each other again, and then she walked away and disappeared around the corner. I went back to the café for another drink. I never saw Anne again.

4

TIME

*It is the road that teaches us the best
way to get there, and the road enriches
us as we walk its length.*

—PAULO COELHO,
THE PILGRIMAGE

I left Logroño in the morning to walk alone for the next week. Each day took me to another town or village—Navarrete, Nájera, Azofra, Santo Domingo de la Calzada, Belorado, Villafranca Montes de Orca, and San Juan de Ortega—where I'd meet other pilgrims at the refugios and, perhaps, share a meal or drink. But the walking was a solitary venture, and as happens with solitude, it started to work on my head. It seemed to me the Camino was laying its claim on my psyche.

It was a bit confusing at times. I found I couldn't recall without effort where I'd been three days, four days, or even a week earlier. The process of walking, of putting one foot in front of the other for mile after mile, hour after hour, seemed to force a reset of my normal sense of time, of one day or one event following another in an orderly sequence. For some reason my immediate pre-pilgrimage memories—I'd flown to London, taken a train to Paris, caught another train to Bayonne— were sharp and orderly. But somehow it was harder to keep track in a sequential fashion of what had happened since I left Saint-Jean-Pied-de-Port. The days of walking were a blurred and overlapping collection of landscapes, paths, streets, churches, bars, monuments, and faces. Without my notebooks it was difficult to recall where exactly I'd been or what I'd done or seen or felt on any particular day. It struck me that for one of the few times in my adult life, I was living in the present. I

gave no thought to what had happened yesterday and what might happen tomorrow. Only the Camino, this day, this hour, was real.[1]

That reality was, of course, often irritating. It was difficult to maintain my newfound stoicism of "just walking" when the frequent rain
left me cold and wet. I had spells of homesickness, wondering how my
wife and son were doing, whether the bills were paid and the doors
locked at night. And, as if I needed reminding, there was the constant
soreness of my feet and legs, although fortunately no other outbreak of
blisters. But at the same time, each day's walk added another image to
the kaleidoscope: a fine meal, a distant vista, sudden birdsong, a Romanesque or Gothic church. I think the Brazilian author Paulo Coelho,
who walked the Camino in 1986, captured well what I experienced, or
more precisely what I felt, in those days of solitude: "After so much
time walking the Road to Santiago, the Road to Santiago began to 'walk
me.'"[2]

Certainly, there was always something to remind me not to take
the Camino lightly. Just as in the Middle Ages, pilgrims still die on the
Camino. I sometimes saw flowers or small crosses marking a spot beside the pilgrimage route. One morning I sheltered from the rain beneath the Romanesque portico of a graveyard outside Navarrete. A
plaque on the wall of the cemetery compound, inscribed in Spanish
and Dutch, commemorated the death of a young Belgian woman killed
in a car accident while cycling to Santiago. It urged passing pilgrims
to offer a prayer. "Peregrino, rez una oración en memoria de Alice de
Graemer, que falleció el 3 7 1985"—Pilgrim, say a prayer in memory of
Alice de Graemer, who died here on 3 July 1985. The inscription also
invited prayer in memory of all pilgrims who died on the Way.[3] And
so I prayed.

I'd read that many of the deaths on the Camino seemed to involve
middle-aged men, such as the German cyclist on his way to Santiago
who suffered a heart attack in the mountains of El Bierzo. An iron
bicycle sculpture at El Acebo, near León, honors his memory.[4] Then
there was a story I heard during my walk about Guillermo Watt, a
Dutchman who died of a heart attack only a few kilometers outside
Santiago—while his wife waited for him in the city.

Sometimes I came across skeletons or desiccated carcasses of animals. They were mostly hares, but a couple of times I saw the bodies of

dogs, their eyes obscured by flies. Once I spotted the carcass of a sheep in a field just off the road, its belly ripped open, exposing the entrails. Another time, the sound of splashing made me pause at a roadside well. Peering over the edge, I saw the pale bellies of half a dozen frogs floating on the water. But not all of them were dead. Two frogs tried repeatedly to grip the slippery stones. I was tempted to lean over the lip of the well to try to scoop them out with my hat, but the image of myself falling into the well restrained me. I watched them struggle until, exhausted, they fell back and sank beneath the surface. The image of those pale bellies bobbing in the dark water lingered in my mind for a long while.

I encountered numerous dogs along the Camino. It sometimes seemed that every village had a dog that became hysterical at the sight of a passing pilgrim. I was thankful their owners generally kept them on chains. Even so, the sudden and unexpected barking as I passed by on some narrow street was sufficiently startling to set my heart racing. It was enough to keep me mindful of their potential presence. The American writer Jack Hitt highlighted the pilgrim's fear of dogs in a decidedly comedic account of his pilgrimage with a reference to a wooden bas-relief in the pilgrim museum at Roncesvalles. The artifact showed a pack of dogs attacking a pilgrim. One animal had pinned the hapless man to the ground, its snarling teeth about to bite down on his screaming face. "The pilgrim's expression of primal horror was finely carved and particularly memorable," Hitt wrote in recounting his own mad-dog encounter.[5]

Hitt's account, which I'd read as part of my pre-Camino research, set me up for my own dog encounter long before it happened. Like many a would-be pilgrim, I fretted at the possibility of a dog attack even though I told myself such things were just too "medieval" to happen nowadays.[6] But it does happen, even to celebrities. Shirley MacLaine had recounted meeting a pack of snarling dogs. But when she claimed to have fended them off by sending "the largest love-imbued heart image I could muster," I found it difficult to take her seriously.[7]

The only time I feared for my life during the pilgrimage was outside Nájera. I was stumbling down a hill past a farm—a sheep farm, judging from the smell—when I heard loud barking behind me. I swung around to see four large dogs coming straight toward me. Unlike Shirley

MacLaine, I couldn't muster much compassion for my attackers. As the dogs charged, I reacted like any normal animal. The adrenaline kicked in, the hair on the back of my neck bristled, and my face took on a snarling look. I wasn't thinking. I was in full fight-or-flight mode. My savior was the collapsible high-tech Hillmaster walking stick with its nice sharp tungsten tip. I growled back and slashed the Hillmaster at the dogs as I slowly retreated, kicking myself mentally for leaving my large knife at the bottom of my pack. Barking furiously, the dogs advanced, careful to stay beyond the reach of my thrashing stick. If they'd been smarter they would have encircled me and taken me down like a helpless sheep. My eyes flicked from one dog to another, trying to determine which one was the leader. Get him, I figured, and the rest would back away. I was going to shove my walking stick down the mangy beast's throat, if I could.

I didn't get the chance. As suddenly as it began, the attack ended. The dogs stopped and let me continue my retreat unmolested, urging me on with the occasional bark. I had, I guessed, moved beyond the bounds of their territorial imperative. I stopped, too. I was breathing as if I'd run a marathon. My hands and arms trembled. I rubbed my face to get the muscles to relax and took some deep breaths to get my heart rate down.

In his account, Hitt disclosed how an instinct to kill had overwhelmed him and made him charge the dogs. I wasn't that brave or, perhaps, so stoked on adrenaline. Still, I sympathized with his inclination. I stayed on my side of whatever psychic boundary existed between the dogs and me, but in my imagination I pulled a rifle out of my knapsack and shot them. In reality, I opted for demonstrating which of us was the superior species. It was my most ridiculous moment on the Camino.

After the encounter, I should have just turned and walked away. Instead, I hopped around grunting and gesticulating and making monkey faces at the dogs. Presumably my tree-climbing hominid ancestors had reacted in a similar fashion when they'd cheated death at the jaws of some saber-toothed tiger; they would have understood my behavior. The dogs certainly seemed to understand, and were they ever insulted. They didn't charge, but they barked with renewed frenzy. We had a stand-off. I stared at the dogs, and the dogs stared at me. I grunted.

They barked. After a while it dawned on me that I was behaving in a most absurd manner and would look like an idiot if the farmer who owned the dogs showed up and saw me tormenting his beloved beasts.

Summoning my dignity, I departed, sauntering away with as much nonchalance as my trembling legs could manage. Of course, I wanted to have the last word. "Vete a la mierda, perros estúpidos," I shouted as I thrust my stick upright in the commonly used gesture. I was sure the dogs got the message because they went into full-tilt barking again.

Long-distance runners refer to a "runner's high"—a state of euphoria achieved after long effort. Pilgrims achieve something similar. I hit my pilgrim's high in the hills of La Rioja, passing roving herds of sheep and goats and villages of adobe-style houses with red pantile roofs. The steady rhythm of my footsteps, the swaying rasp of the pack on my back, the metronomic tap of my walking stick—they all worked to quiet the chatter in my head. And in the lull, the door of memory creaked open. Long-ago lovers and friends, schoolmates and traveling companions, some of whom I hadn't seen since childhood, came vividly to mind. I remembered Harley and Chuck, Pat and Rock, Carol and Maxine, Jane and Donna, David and Kirk, Gillian and Jolayne—whatever happened to them?

My days of solitary walking also lifted the latch on a psychic cellar door where, unbeknownst to my conscious self, I'd hoarded all sorts of treasures and keepsakes, along with a fair amount of pop-culture residue.[8] If I wasn't conversing with long-lost friends, then I was tuning in to some subconscious radio station where an eternally youthful DJ spun the golden oldies in perpetuity. I bounced along, warbling lyrics from the Beatles and the Beach Boys, Elvis Presley and Roy Orbison, Del Shannon and the Four Seasons. Every now and then, however, the mental needle kept getting stuck on the records from my childhood: "The Battle of New Orleans," "Tom Dooley," "Sink the Bismarck," "Moon River." Strolling beside a vineyard, I sang, "From a Jack to a King, from loneliness to old memories, I played my heart and won a Queen." Stepping over fresh sheep dung, I yodeled, "The night has a thousand eyes and a thousand eyes can't help but see if you are true to me." Splashing across a puddle, I crooned, "Moon River, wider than a mile, I'm crossing you in style some day."[9]

Those songs evoked images from the early 1960s when my family had lived in Inuvik. I remembered the small crystal radio receiver my father had built for me. Most of the time, all I'd been able to pick up was the local CBC station. But sometimes I'd tuned in to radio stations as far away as Alberta and Alaska. On rare occasions I'd heard Russian voices, depending, as my dad had explained, on conditions in the upper atmosphere and the way the radio waves bounced. It had seemed a marvel to me as a boy that I could hear voices and songs from so far away, and I'd daydreamed of someday going to all those places.

The sudden images of those childhood years in Inuvik, so sharp in my mind, stopped me in my tracks. Physically, I stood in the middle of a muddy, rutted path along the Camino de Santiago in northern Spain. Mentally, I was thousands of miles away in a small town above the Arctic Circle in northern Canada. I hadn't thought of my father's homemade radio—a semiconductor diode, a tuning coil of copper wire, antennae taped to the bedroom window, and a jack for the earpiece, glued to a small block of wood—for years. But standing on the Camino I saw myself as a boy, curled up in bed, half asleep, with the sounds of the world in my head. The memory was incredibly vivid. I could see my bedroom, the checked brown and beige bedspread, the reddish colonial-style bedside table where my radio sat next to the lamp, the pictures of astronauts and rockets on the walls, and my model of a Gemini capsule hanging from the ceiling.

I walked on, lost in memory, as images from the past ebbed and flowed with each step. For a while I was a small boy again, standing in the back seat of our family's 1949 burgundy-colored Dodge DeSoto—this was long before seatbelts—and looking over my father's shoulder through the windshield as the farm fields and telephone poles whipped past on a summer weekend drive from Red Deer to Drumheller. Bobby Vinton's "Blue Velvet" played on the radio. The song was so audible in my head that for a moment I could have sworn it was playing on a radio somewhere in the vineyard I was passing.

There were other treasures in my memory chest, too. I nattered poetry from half-forgotten English classes: lines by Matthew Arnold, a fragment of Milton, a phrase from Eliot. "In the sea of life enisled, / With echoing straits between us thrown, / Dotting the shoreless watery wild, / We mortal millions live alone." "The world was all before them, where to choose / Their place of rest, and Providence their guide. / They, hand in hand, with wandering steps and slow, / Through Eden took their solitary way." "We shall not cease from exploration / And the end of all our exploring / Will be to arrive where we started / And know the place for the first time."[10] I was delighted I'd actually absorbed something from my university years and even from my high school English teacher, Leon Logie.

And so I walked across the Spanish countryside, jabbering lyrics and poems and revisiting other times and places in my past. In those moments my pilgrimage acquired a significance I hadn't anticipated. I remembered Michel Mallet, the *hospitalero* in Saint-Jean-Pied-de-Port, asking whether my pilgrimage was religiously, spiritually, or culturally motivated as he issued my *credencial*. I'd been uncertain how to reply. I couldn't honestly claim a religious motive; my Catholicism had long ago lapsed. To assert a spiritual motive was too New Age for my cultivated skepticism. I'd opted for "cultural." At least it was better than "tourist." But as I walked and mumbled the poetry and songs of my past and imagined conversations with old friends, it occurred to me that perhaps I deserved an upgrade to the spiritual category.

The word "spirit" comes from the Latin *spiritus*, which is a translation of the Greek word *pneuma*, and it refers to that which breathes life into a body, that which gives meaning and purpose to life. It seemed to me those moments of intense memory granted me a glimpse of my own spirit, hinted at what gave my life a sense of meaning and purpose. Graduation to religious faith, to belief in some ultimate or metaphysical reality, might be unavailable, I thought, but maybe I could find a sense of meaning in the intimacies and revelations of memory.

My mental rummaging wasn't unusual. The triggering of half-forgotten memories is a well-known psychological phenomenon of pilgrimage. Nancy Frey referred to the Camino's "out of time quality" in her 1998 study: "While journeying through this different time and place, pilgrims find that long-forgotten memories surface; memories of family members and friends, childhood places, secrets or painful circumstances. These new perceptions often take people to internal places not before visited."[11]

I mentioned my experience to other pilgrims—two balding, broad-shouldered Germans, Peter Ainsler and Meinhoff Schleyer—with whom I had dinner one night in the Bar Seville in Azofra. "That's a good sign," Peter said. "That's what should happen. The Camino is having an effect on you."

Peter and Meinhoff were brothers-in-law. Both were in their early sixties and had recently retired from engineering careers. They were walking the Camino because they felt at loose ends and wanted to test themselves physically and, perhaps, reacquaint themselves with their lapsed Catholicism.

"The Camino is a simple life," Meinhoff commented. "You walk. You eat. You sleep. You forget about everything, except what's important."

"I was an altar boy," Peter said, "but I haven't been in church for many years. Funerals and weddings, but not for confession. I've been thinking about returning to the Church." As he downed his beer he added with a laugh, "I have much to confess."

I'd met the Germans, along with a Dane by the name of Henrik Friediger, the previous evening in the refugio at Navarrete. We'd taken over the Los Arcos bar for a lengthy and sometimes raucous meal after the day's walking. Inevitably the talk turned to motivations for walking the Camino.

"Everybody in my office walks around with a Palm Pilot and goes to endless meetings. I don't carry a Palm Pilot on the Camino. There's no stress. That's why I like it," said Henrik, summing it up for everyone.

In the Age of Faith, men and women journeyed to Santiago to be closer to God and to atone for their sins. In our faithless era, we go on a pilgrimage to relieve stress. No wonder some refer to the Camino as *la ruta de la terapia*, the therapy route. A pilgrimage journey might unlock a treasure chest of memories, but it can also offer salve for the wounds of daily life.[12]

The religious dimension of the Camino could not be ignored, however, even if I were so inclined, as I discovered a couple of days later in Santo Domingo de la Calzada. Following the yellow arrows through the streets of the town one afternoon, I arrived at the Catedral del Salvador y Virgen de la Asunción, a huge stone church that dates to the twelfth century with a mix of Romanesque and Gothic styles. Its baroque tower was built later and stands strangely separate across the street from the main building. I wandered around the church, admiring the stonework, the statues, and the sculpture, especially the apse with its figures depicting a mix of human vices and saintly deeds—a glutton stuffing his face, a figure sharing his cape with a pilgrim.

The cathedral interior was even more impressive. I spent at least an hour quietly wandering around, stroking the ornately carved pillars that rose up into the dim heights of the vaulted ceiling, staring at the golden floor-to-ceiling altar, admiring the beauty of the chapels and clerestory. I tried to puzzle out the meaning of the allegorical motifs that decorated the pillars and friezes. I figured out that one pillar showed God the Father holding His infant Son in His arms as He stood beside the Virgin Mary. Or at least that was how I understood it, appalled at my ignorance of my Judeo-Christian heritage.

I studied the panels depicting the life of Santo Domingo, an early eleventh-century hermit who dedicated himself to serving pilgrims, building roads and bridges, and providing food and shelter. His tomb was in the southern part of the transept. I stood for a few moments looking at the sculpture of his reclining figure. Bas-relief scenes from his life adorned the side of the tomb. His crypt was underneath. I ran my hand along the saint's stone shoulder. It was cold to the touch.

I was about to leave when I heard the cackling of chickens. For a moment I thought it was an auditory hallucination, but looking up at the transept opposite Santo Domingo's tomb I saw an ornate cage containing two chickens, a rooster and a hen so far as I could tell. I'd forgotten Santo Domingo's most famous legend: the story of the resurrected chickens.

According to the twelfth-century tale, a young man accompanying his mother and father on a pilgrimage to Santiago rejected the amorous advances of a local serving girl. Humiliated by the rejection, she slipped a piece of silver into his wallet while he slept. After the family departed, she denounced him to the authorities as a thief. Tried and convicted, he was sent to the gallows. The grieving parents continued on to Santiago, but on their way back home they stopped at the gallows to pray. Imagine their surprise when their son, still hanging from the gibbet, spoke. He told them that thanks to the miraculous support of Santo Domingo—literal support, apparently—he wasn't strangled, but they needed to get the judge who had condemned him to cut him down. The judge, about to sit down to his chicken dinner, mocked the parents' story: "The truth of your tale is as likely as these two chickens being able to stand up and crow." Miraculously, the roasted and feather-less birds did exactly that. Most impressed, the judge duly ordered the young man restored to his parents. Ever since, or so the legend goes, locals have kept two chickens in the cathedral.

As word of the miracle spread, pilgrims started collecting the feath-ers that fell out of the coop and tucking them into their caps as a sign that Santo Domingo had blessed their pilgrimage. Of course I dis-missed the story as medieval nonsense, but I still looked on the stone floor beneath the coop for my own feather. I could hear the chickens clucking away, but there were no feathers for me. I wondered if they were laughing at me.

They might well have been. It struck me that my inability to com-prehend the meaning of all that I had seen in the cathedral, its symbolic objects and allegorical carvings, was both a reproach to my modern education and a judgment on my theological ignorance. How could I know anything of faith when I understood nothing, intellectually or emotionally, of the expressions of that faith? I was like the cynical, ill-informed narrator in Philip Larkin's famous poem "Church Going," who wandered into an empty church prepared to dismiss the "brass and stuff" at "the holy end" only to find himself strangely drawn to the place, aware of "a hunger" that he, the modern skeptical rationalist taught to regard religion as superstition, could never satisfy.[13] I left the cathedral with the clucking of the chickens echoing in my head.

Behind the cathedral, in the Plaza Mayor, I found a bench beneath a large beech tree and sat there debating whether I wanted to walk any further that day. I noticed groups of young women coming into the plaza. They gathered in small clusters beneath a long arcade that ran the length of the ancient town hall across the plaza from where I sat. I wondered what they were doing or waiting for until, suddenly, the plaza filled with children laughing, shouting, jumping, and running. School was out!

I preferred this tableau, the holiness of the everyday world—in this case, watching children play—to that of the next world offered in the cathedral. I closed my eyes to listen to their laughter bounce off the walls of the surrounding buildings. I heard the delighted shriek of a girl, the exuberant yell of a boy, and above me, barely audible amid the sounds of the children, the chirping of birds.

I opened my eyes and looked up, trying to find the nest in the tree. I couldn't see it, but I spotted a large yellow cat sitting on a low bough, staring up into the canopy of leaves. I monitored the cat's movements, thinking I'd chase it away with my Hillmaster if it went after the nest. But the cat, perhaps deciding it was too risky a climb, eventually jumped to the ground and padded away. I was relieved. I would have looked quixotically foolish to these children if I'd started attacking a tree with my walking stick.

When the cathedral bell struck the hour, I saw that my watch said 4 p.m. I decided it was too late to walk any more that day. I needed a place to sleep and left the square to the children. I found a room at the Pensión del Río on Calle Etchegoyen, a couple of blocks from the cathedral. After washing socks and underwear, I showered and changed and went out looking for food. I wanted fried chicken but settled for a couple of ham *bocadillos* and a bottle of Estrella Damm at the Bar Chomin, near the main bus stop on the Plaza de San Jerónimo Hermosilla. It was an old-fashioned place with a long zinc bar on one side of the narrow room and beveled mirrors on the wall behind the bar. A row of wooden tables and chairs lined the gray-tiled opposite wall. Cigarette butts littered the floor. It was my kind of place. I spent the evening at a table by the window, soaking up the smoky atmosphere, observing the locals come and go, and watching episodes of *The Simpsons* in Spanish on the television above the bar. It hardly mattered that I didn't understand the words. I was comfortable and oddly content to listen to the indecipherable chatter of the other patrons and let the memories drift as they pleased. I ordered another beer.

5

GRATITUDE

Knowing is a road.
—ANNE CARSON,
PLAINWATER

I still felt content when I walked out of Santo Domingo in the morning, if a little fuzzy in the head from the succession of beers the night before. When I left my hotel, I lost sight of the yellow arrows and ended up wandering back and forth along some street until an elderly man emerged from his shop and gestured toward a maze of alleys, "El Camino, el Camino." "Gracias, señor," I shouted as I headed up the street in the direction he indicated. When I spotted a much-faded yellow arrow, I looked back to wave at the old man to show him I'd found my way. I saw him make the sign of the cross as he watched me from the doorway. The gesture probably came automatically to him, but it startled me. However uncertain I was of my motives for being on the Camino, and however flawed my performance, he took it on faith that I was a sincere and penitent pilgrim.

Three days after the old man's blessing I was feeling rather penitential when I arrived in Burgos. I was staggering with fatigue, and my legs ached with each step. The twenty-five-kilometer stretch to Burgos from San Juan de Ortega, where I'd stayed the previous night, had cut through a long stretch of unpopulated and hilly woodland where snow still lay on the ground and the wind blew cold and wet through the trees. My right leg, in particular, which until then had offered only odd twinges of protest, issued some serious complaints. Every few steps a jolt of pain rocketed up from the back of my heel to my knee. By the time I reached Castanares, a suburb of Burgos, I was limping badly.

I surrendered to the pain and took a bus into Burgos, walking—stumbling would be more accurate—the last few hundred yards from the bus station to the Hostal Conde de Miranda, just off Calle de Madrid near where it crosses the Río Arlanzón. That night over dinner at the Bar Goano, I made some calculations: I'd walked—if you didn't count the occasional bus or taxi—nearly three hundred kilometers, averaging between twenty-two and twenty-five kilometers a day. Not marathon standards, but I was gradually getting to where I was going. Perhaps I was learning the Zen injunction: just walk. But prudence dictated a day off, which proved to be a good decision. I woke up in the middle of the night with my right leg throbbing. I sat up, turned on the bedside lamp, and found a mottled rash stretching from my ankle to halfway up my calf. I hardly knew what to think. I could deal with blisters, but a bout of tendonitis was a scary prospect. If it got too bad, I'd be unable to continue my pilgrimage. But I was too tired to think about that, and I pulled the covers back over my legs, lay down, and fell asleep again, figuring I couldn't do much until morning anyway. Even then, there wasn't much I could do except wrap my calf and ankle with surgical tape and promise to go gently on it for the day. Limping or not, I wasn't going to miss seeing one of Spain's loveliest cities.

Burgos is the city of El Cid Campeador, the Moor-slayer of the *Reconquista*, second only to Santiago himself as a Spanish national hero. During the Spanish Civil War, Generalísimo Franco adopted the city as his temporary capital. I limped along Calle de Madrid and across the river, then walked along the Paseo del Espolón, admiring its fine old buildings and wide boulevards with their pollarded trees and topiary hedges. The croaking frogs on the banks of the milky green river were almost loud enough to drown out the early morning traffic. I wandered through the narrow streets until I found a restaurant where I could have my breakfast of churros and café con leche. Afterward, I located a *farmacia* and replenished my medical supplies and then bought some postcards at a street-side kiosk. After a slow, sauntering exploration of the streets, I found a quiet bar with a nice view of the esplanade along the river where I could rest my leg. There I could also indulge in the occasional *chato*, a small glass of the house red wine, while I scribbled greetings to friends and family and caught up on my pilgrimage notes.

In the afternoon, I spent a couple of hours exploring the Burgos Cathedral on Calle de Madrid. With its forest of spires, elaborate carvings depicting myths and biblical stories, star-vaulted domes, and a gilded double staircase known as the Golden Steps, the cathedral is one of Spain's great Gothic structures, dating to the early thirteenth century. There was too much to absorb: 19 chapels, 38 altars, 58 pillars on which the naves rest, and 38 interior arches. Still, I admired the monumental metal brazier in the main sacristy, which, according to my guidebook, has burned without pause since the seventeenth century. I took my time behind the apse, studying the five almost lifelike medallions with their stone carvings of scenes from Calvary. They were so realistic that I half convinced myself the artist had captured Christ's muscles going slack at the moment of his death. It was hard to imagine any Resurrection after such a death.

I had to admire, even envy, the faith that could produce something as beautiful as this cathedral. While made of stone, it looks like a monument of filigree lace reaching for the sky. With its flying buttresses, ribbed vaulting, stained-glass windows, sculptured facades, and soaring spires, it symbolizes a meeting of the human and the divine. Before I left, I lit a candle and sat in a pew to watch it burn, enjoying the cool echoing quiet of the sanctuary. When I walked outside, I felt calm and somehow cleansed.

I ate dinner in the Bar Miranda and watched a bullfight on television before returning to my room for an early night. Regardless of the swelling and the soreness of my leg, I was determined to return to the Camino in the morning.

Beyond Burgos, the Camino crossed the dustiest, flattest, most windswept, and for some the most monotonous landscape in Spain. This was the *meseta*, the Tierra de Campos, that stretches across the middle of Spain. The Spanish call the *meseta* the "roof of the world." In the summer it would be sun-baked and parched, but in the early spring it was a lush, undulating panorama of green.

I cheated a bit when leaving Burgos by taking a taxi twelve kilometers to Rabé de las Calzadas. After a maze of suburban roads and industrial wasteland, the cabbie dropped me at an intersection where the road turned into a footpath that cut across a green field. It was the middle of nowhere, or so it seemed to me.

"¿El Camino? ¿Aquí?" I asked the driver. He nodded. We both got out of the car, and he helped me shoulder my pack. I gave him a hefty tip on top of the fare. "Gracias," he said as he got back in his car. He nodded farewell and wished me a *buen Camino*. "¡Ultreya!" I watched him drive away to the city, leaving me alone in the empty land beneath a gray sky that threatened rain.

Two hours later, I hobbled as fast as my aching legs allowed through the tiny village of Hornillos del Camino to find shelter as the clouds finally let loose. I ended up huddling beneath the arcade across the front of a church that dominated the town square. The church had once been an important pilgrimage stop, with a hospital and a Benedictine monastery. The monks had long since disappeared, and so it seemed had everyone else. The streets were empty and the windows of the houses shuttered. I sat on a stone bench against the wall and watched the rain pound the cobblestones out in the square in a loud and constant drumming. At times the rain came down so hard and furious that it ricocheted upward to form a knee-high curtain of water. I closed my eyes to focus on the sound, enjoying the way it seemed to obliterate all thought.

I must have nodded off because I didn't hear the approach of another pilgrim until the thump of a pack on the ground startled me. I opened my eyes to see a man pulling off his dripping hat and poncho. To my surprise, it was Gerard, the Belgian pilgrim and former soldier whom I'd met nearly three weeks earlier in Saint-Jean-Pied-de-Port. He was surprised to see me, too. For him to have caught up with me after all my buses and taxis meant he'd been covering quite a distance every day, certainly more than I had.

We shook hands and asked after each other's pilgrimage. Gerard pulled an orange out of his pack and shared it as we chatted. But I could tell Gerard was not really there with me. Soldiers say you can tell a man who has been in combat by the faraway look in his eyes. They call it the thousand-yard stare. Gerard had the pilgrim version of that mesmerized look. Eventually we ran out of words and just sat watching the rain. I suspected that whereas I was sheltering from the weather, hoping it would break soon, Gerard was simply taking a break. He would walk, rain or not. The weather didn't matter to him. "Rain or snow, it doesn't matter, you just keep walking," he'd advised when I first met him. I sensed he wanted to get moving and was merely being companionable in lingering with me.

Just then I heard more footsteps, and who came in out of the rain but Henrik the Dane. If I had welcomed Gerard's arrival, I was downright cheered by the sight of Henrik. I introduced him to Gerard, and they talked for a few minutes. But Gerard took Henrik's arrival as a reason to leave. We again shook hands, wishing each other a *buen Camino*, and then Gerard disappeared into the rain. I never saw him again.

Henrik and I caught up on Camino gossip. He'd seen Peter and Meinhoff outside Burgos. As I had, he not only had spent a day exploring the city but also had taken a taxi to Rabé de las Calzadas. He, too, was content to wait until the rain had eased before returning to the Camino. We chatted back and forth about our respective pilgrimages.

Henrik was a fifty-four-year-old senior bureaucrat in Denmark's Ministry of Education, primarily engaged in forming educational policy. His first pilgrimage had been in 1992. He'd walked and bused 470 kilometers from Burgos to Santiago. In 1994, he and his son, then twelve, had walked from Roncesvalles to Santiago in thirty-two days. Two years later, he and his wife had completed a highlights-of-the-Camino trek through Galicia. He'd traveled the whole route himself again in 1998, walking and taking trains and buses. When I met him he was using his four-week holiday to walk from Pamplona to Santiago.

The rain finally ceased or, more accurately, became a light drizzle. I said inquiringly, "Ultreya?" Henrik nodded. We donned our rain jackets and packs, and grabbing our walking sticks we returned to the Camino. It was hard slogging. The rain finally stopped, but the wind had picked up, coming directly at us out of the west, forcing us to lean into it. The ochre mud clung to our boots, making the walk even harder. I was the slower walker, but Henrik stayed with me until I urged him to go on. We would meet in Hontanas for lunch.

The trail stretched out in front of me like an unfurling ribbon, rising and falling with the contours of the land. I could see far ahead. Henrik would drop out of sight behind a roll in the land and then reappear as I crested a slope. Occasionally, he stopped to look back to see how I was doing. I'd wave, and he'd walk on. Like the yellow arrows, his presence was reassuring. Eventually, though, Henrik disappeared, and I was alone on the trail with the gray-bellied clouds scudding low over the *meseta.*

The landscape seemed to change with each step, yielding different species of flowers, different mixtures of rock and pebble, and even varying densities of mud. I noticed how the surfaces of the Camino itself—hard or soft, smooth or sharp—changed, albeit in subtle ways. Walking on asphalt was different from walking on an earthen path. When my feet pounded the unyielding pavement, the walking was monotonous and dull and somehow irritating. But on the unpaved paths, there were constant surprises that demanded attention: a rut to leap, a rivulet to cross, a puddle to sidestep. I found myself staring at even ordinary features of the scenery: distant hills that looked like shaven heads, a copse of stunted trees silhouetted against the sky, a cluster of boulders covered with sun-blackened lichen, a bright strip of poppies or wild lupine in a ditch, clouds like distant ships sailing across the horizon.[1]

A few kilometers outside Hontanas, just before the Arroyo del Garbanzuelo, I came to a crossroads. There were no yellow arrows painted on boulders or tree trunks to indicate which direction to take. Uncertain, I stood at the edge of the path, leaning on my walking stick to ease the strain on my legs, and gradually became aware of how quiet it was. Normally, the crunch of my boots, the flapping of my jacket, or the rasp of my backpack filled my ears. But standing still, I noticed the wind had died down and given way to silence. I listened, looking across the land as it stretched far beyond me, and waited, as if for something to happen.

Suddenly there came a memory. It was of a summer when I was a boy, maybe eight or nine years old, and I was walking alone on a prairie road outside my hometown of Hanna, Alberta. The sun was hot on my head and shoulders. Cicadas chirped in the roadside ditches. Grasshoppers jumped around my legs. Beneath a huge vacant sky, the air itself seemed to hum in the heat of the day. The image of myself standing beneath that colossal sky was so visually intense that for a few seconds I seemed to be in two places at once: a boy standing on the Alberta prairie and a much older version of that boy leaning on a walking stick on the Spanish *meseta.* The vision held me entranced. It seemed to me that I needed only to step forward and I would pass through some barely perceptible barrier and be my young self again, a boy returned to that long-lost summer I'd spent with my grandparents.

A burst of birdsong shattered the image and snapped me back to the present. A flock of warblers, like a collection of question marks against the sky, swooped down on the boulders covered with lichen. Suddenly everything—the vast land, the sheltering sky, the rain-puddled path, the pungent earth—shimmered with brilliance as a gap in the clouds allowed a wide shaft of sunlight to fall on the *meseta*. It lasted for only a few seconds before the clouds closed up again, but in those moments the whole world seemed to shimmer.

I was left blinking and wondering what had happened. Some half-remembered lines from R. S. Thomas came to mind: "Moments of great calm, / Kneeling before an altar / . . . waiting for the God." The rest was lost to me except for the poem's last line: "The meaning is in the waiting."[2]

I waited for a few moments longer, hoping for another vision, until I heard the warblers again. The spell was broken. I had miles to go and a luncheon date to keep.

I found Henrik in a bar in Hontanas. I was tempted to tell him about my experience, but I wasn't sure how to explain it. Endorphins maybe? Hallucination born of solitude? I didn't know, so I kept it to myself. In any case, the sight of Henrik enjoying a tureen of soup and a large jug of wine reminded me that I was hungry. I joined him at a battered wooden table hemmed in by a hodge-podge of canned goods, bags of grain, farming implements, pieces of machinery, and stacks of worn tires. I was too hungry to worry about the decor, much less whether the place had a health inspector's approval. I dug into the soup after checking to see there was nothing thriving in the chipped bowl the bar's owner, Victorino Díez, handed to me.

A short, stocky man, Díez was a jack-of-all-trades and well known on the pilgrim route for his garage-cum-restaurant. Besides food, he also offered taxi service. While we ate, Henrik arranged to have our packs delivered to the refugio in Castrojeriz, where we planned to stay that night. I was amazed at how much easier it was to walk without that burden. Beyond Hontanas, the Camino followed a narrow tarmac road lined by tall Lombardy poplars. The air smelled clean from the morning's rain. There was little traffic, and Henrik and I could walk and talk.

"My job has a lot of stress," Henrik said when I asked him why he'd walked the Camino so many times. "Every day I have to juggle five or six balls in the air at once. Here, on the Camino, I only have to juggle one ball—walking—and if I drop it once in a while, no problem, who cares? When I'm here I forget about the work. It all disappears. There are only the villages and the land and the walking."

The *hospitalero* at the refugio in Castrojeriz turned out to be an officious jerk. The ground floor was already full, but he refused to allow anyone upstairs. The lower section was cramped and damp, and the bunk beds were set back in tiny cell-like alcoves off a passageway. As if that wasn't bad enough, the atmosphere in the refugio made the situation even worse, and I don't mean solely in terms of odor. Nationalism prevailed over any sense of European community. Germans, Belgians, Spaniards, and French staked out their territories, setting up defensive perimeters with socks, underwear, and wet towels, and sending the clear message that only those of like nationality were welcomed into each enclave. The lack of facilities didn't help matters. There was only one shower, and no hot water. Pilgrims shouted about who was in line ahead of whom.

Henrik and I didn't stick around to see if war broke out. We retreated to a bar for a drink. Henrik suggested we find a taxi and proceed to the next village, Itero de la Vega. That was fine with me, and half an hour later we unfolded our sleeping bags in a dry and all but empty refugio. Only two other pilgrims were there, one of whom was Charles Henri, the retired businessman I'd met in Zubiri on my second day on the Camino. We greeted each other like long-lost relatives. The other pilgrim was Jamey Austin, a blond-haired and bearded thirty-year-old from near San Francisco. "Boy, am I glad to see you," Jamey said. He was sitting on his bunk and applying ice to one of his ankles. "I haven't spoken English to anyone for a long time."

Jamey's legs were swollen and mottled by a rash, much like the one I had in Burgos. Jamey explained that he'd started on the Camino after hearing about it while traveling elsewhere in Spain. "I knew I had to do it. It's been a great experience. I love it. Except I've been doing forty,

forty-five kilometers a day for the past couple of weeks, just motoring, you know, and I think I've done some damage to my tendons." I commiserated and told him about my leg and blister woes, giving him some moleskin and surgical tape to wrap his ankles and heels.

Later, after our showers, the four of us had dinner in a *tasca*, or tavern, near the refugio. Oddly, no one was very talkative. Perhaps our companionable silence was testament to our shared experience. As Charles put it, "The spirit is changing, c'est tout."

Back at the refugio we found another pilgrim settling in: a novice priest. He'd wrapped his feet with strips of cloth so only his toes showed. Blood stains spotted the bindings. I didn't see any boots or other footwear, but there was no sign of limping on the priest's part. I fell asleep wondering if there was a relation between having faith and not feeling pain.

Jamey, Charles, and the priest were gone when I woke up. Henrik and I took our time before setting out. We were heading for Villalcázar de Sirga, about twenty-five kilometers away. It would be easy walking across flat land. I enjoyed walking with Henrik. With his experience of the Camino, he knew where to stay, what to see, and what to avoid.

For some reason I never discovered, Henrik was fond of black spirituals, and we walked along singing "Nobody knows the trouble I've seen" or "Go tell it on the mountain, over the hill and everywhere." I tried to teach him "Tom Dooley" and "Moon River." When we weren't singing we talked about Denmark's social welfare system compared to Canada's, the ruinous weight of taxation in both countries—the kind of things that were supposedly important. Except on the Camino, they didn't seem important. I realized I hadn't thought about the mortgage, the stock market, or even my job for days. "We're just two over-taxed, footsore, middle-aged conservatives on a pilgrimage," Henrik said. His droll tone was hilarious. We had to stop until our laughter subsided.

We took a break after crossing a series of irrigation channels to Boadilla del Camino where we drank from a *rollo*, or water fountain, that dated to Roman times. While we rested, I took off my boots for an inspection. The rash had faded and the swelling subsided, but there were a couple of small blisters. I hauled out the moleskin and Compeed.

In Frómista, we toured the Romanesque Church of San Martín

with its hundreds of carved figures of animals, monsters, and humans—some performing sexual acts that would give modern-day pornographers pause and induce hysteria in the animal rights crowd. In the fields beyond Población de Campos, we saw three dogs chase down and kill a hare in a rout of dust. In Villalcázar de Sirga, we were joined once again by Charles. We stayed in the refugio and persuaded the parish priest to give us a tour of the Church of Santa María La Blanca with its painted tombs of a Templar knight and his wife.

The next day we reached Carrión de los Condes, and I was once again having difficulty walking. Tendonitis, I figured. The rash I'd had in Burgos had faded, but my heels and ankles flared with pain by the time I'd walked for maybe two or three hours. We found a bar in Carrión. Over café con leche Henrik suggested that I take the bus to León. The ride would give my tendons a day off without losing three or four days' walking. "You want to look after that leg," he said. "There are many ways to travel the Camino. Everybody does it in the way that suits them." I was sorry to lose Henrik's company. "Maybe we'll meet in Santiago," I said.

Outside, Henrik gave me a hug, a gesture I couldn't remember receiving from another man except my father. We shook hands and he walked away, returning to the *meseta*. I waited for the bus, feeling depressed and disappointed in myself. The sun was shining, and it was a good day for walking. Instead, I went back inside, ordered another coffee, and watched the bartender stack saucers and cups. Suddenly the door swung open, and there was the Brazilian Bombshell, Andrea Libia Lopos, her blond hair flying. She wore tight shorts that highlighted her beautifully tanned and trim legs and a knotted shirt that exposed her midriff and emphasized her breasts. It was lust at first sight for every man in the bar, but I was the one who reaped the benefits of her natural enthusiasm.

"Roberto," she cried, striding across the room and giving me a kiss on both cheeks and a hug.

"Andrea, mi amor," I responded, planting my own kisses and enjoying the hug more than I should have.

Not surprisingly, Andrea had a companion. A thin-haired man, whom I guessed to be in his fifties, followed her into the bar, carrying two backpacks. I ignored him as Andrea and I brought each other up to date, somehow communicating despite her inadequate English and my not-even-inadequate Portuguese. She hadn't seen Anne, but she had seen Elizabeth and Denise in Logroño. Elizabeth's feet were too sore; she'd quit and gone home. José-Luis? Yes, just the other day in Castrojeriz. He seemed fine. As for her, she and her companion, whatever his name was, were taking the bus to Sahagún de Campos, on the way to León.

As we waited for the bus, a husky man in a blue rain jacket arrived. He introduced himself as Ron Chanda, a retired bank executive from Princeton, New Jersey. I introduced him to Andrea, who promptly gave him a hug and kissed his cheeks. He was most impressed and had me take a picture of him with his arms around her shoulders. "Something to show my wife," he said with a grin.

Aboard the bus, Ron told me this was his second walk on the Camino. The previous October he'd walked from Saint-Jean-Pied-de-Port to Burgos. This spring he was going from Burgos to Santiago. "It's the solitude that I like," he said. "When I'm walking I start thinking of things that I don't think about in my regular life, things that, I don't know, seem more important."

By the time the bus pulled into Sahagún, about forty kilometers from León, I'd learned about his family, the daughter he worried about, and the son who was an accountant and of whom he was so proud. The Camino was like that. You met someone for the first time, and within minutes you had a précis of his or her life.[3]

I got off the bus with Ron and Andrea to say goodbye. "Maybe we'll meet again," I said.

"In Santiago," Ron said.

Andrea gave me another one of her marvelous hugs. I told Ron to keep an eye out for Henrik, figuring they'd get along as walking companions if they met up. Then I got back on the bus, expecting never to see them again. About an hour later, I hauled my pack off the bus in León. By that time it was pouring rain.

I'd originally thought I would stay overnight in the city. But all that rain prompted me to want the dry warmth of another bus. I went back into the station to buy a ticket that would take me another twenty-five kilometers to Hospital de Órbigo. Then, as penance for my sloth, I would walk the remaining twenty-odd kilometers to Astorga, rain or shine.

I slept most of the way. By the time the bus arrived I was grateful to see the rain had dwindled to a drizzle. My cheating had helped my legs—especially my right leg. Even a few hours off the road had allowed the swelling to subside. I limped out of town across a long twenty-arch bridge that spans the Río Órbigo, heading toward Astorga. I followed the yellow arrows across a canal and up a green and muddy lane into open country. I don't remember much of that walk beyond the steady drizzle—and the miraculous fate of my legs.

My legs were a constant diversion. The further I walked, the more aware I was of how much they ached. I could feel the pain begin to build and wondered how much more I could take. I trudged along for maybe three hours, grimly putting one foot in front of the other, stabbing my walking stick into the ground and using it to push forward, and feeling the jolts of pain spread from my feet and my knees to my hips. The pain seemed to build and retreat and then build again like an orchestra approaching a crescendo.

It went on like this for what seemed like a long time until, to my surprise, I became aware that the level of pain seemed to have dropped. Slowly and steadily, it finally started to fade. In amazement, I stopped, mentally assessing my body, and wondering if the diminished pain could be true. I started walking again, waiting for the pain to return. It did, but not as bad as before. I halted again for a few minutes before resuming my pace. This time the pain didn't return. It was gone. To be sure, the ache in my feet and legs was always there but not that deep stabbing pain. By the time I reached Astorga I had no pain at all. I was dripping wet and weary, my boots and pants were caked in mud, but I was also nearly euphoric. The pain in my legs had actually gone—not just subsided but gone, disappeared, not there.

Pilgrim lore has it that pain is how the body somaticizes psychological problems.[4] "The sores on your feet are also signs of the disease inside you" was how Edward Stanton put it.[5] I wondered which of my various psychic maladies I'd cured that day. I had blown my pilgrim authenticity by taking a bus, but suddenly I was well with my feet. Not a bad trade-off, I decided. Maybe I'd finally learned to walk. So as I sauntered around Astorga's medieval town center late in the afternoon, caught somewhere between laughing and crying, I sang B. J. Thomas's "Raindrops Keep Falling on My Head."

I checked into a lovely room in the Hotel Gaudí—all blond wood and red-tile flooring. The big double windows looked out over the plaza at the small Church of Santa Marta and the big cathedral with storks' nests on the spires. Across the plaza was the castellated gray-stone Palacio de Gaudí and its pilgrim museum. The building, designed by the eccentric Catalan architect Antoni Gaudí, reminded me of the castle that Tinker Bell flies around while sprinkling fairy dust in the opening credits of *The Wonderful World of Disney.*

I felt as though some fairy or angel had sprinkled me with magic dust. My room's queen-sized bed, thick wool blankets, and gorgeous shower that supplied endless hot water enraptured me. I forced myself to tend to my boots and drape my wet clothes over the chairs to dry before I did anything else. But when I entered the shower, I sat on the floor for a long time and just let the water beat on my chest and legs. I imagined all the pain being washed away and down the drain. Afterward, dressed in my dry spare shirt and pants, I wobbled weak-kneed downstairs to the bar, where to my pleasant surprise I found myself in the midst of a wedding reception. Nobody seemed to object, although among the tuxedos and shimmering dresses I stuck out like a buzzard in a flock of peacocks. Still, I enjoyed myself, happy to lean on the polished wood of the bar with a bottle of Estrella Galicia and a bowl of pretzels, admiring the beautiful women with their glossy hair and bright smiles.

When I finished the beer I went across the hall to the dining room, where I got a table near the large window looking out on the plaza. It was a lovely room with dark wood wainscoting, white tablecloths, and sparking chandeliers hanging on long wrought-iron chains from the high ceiling. I ordered the *sopa castellana*, a spicy stew, and a bottle of Rioja Bordón. I ate slowly, savoring the stew and the vanilla-flavored wine. I had no desire to go anywhere. I leaned back in my green leather chair, lolled the rest of the wine around my palate, watched the other diners, and listened to the clatter of knives and porcelain and the clink of glasses. The dining room Muzak caught my attention with its instrumental versions of 1970s hits: Roberta Flack's "Killing Me Softly with His Song" and Carole King's "I Feel the Earth Move." I thought of a girl I'd loved a long time ago and wondered how her life had turned out. And I thought of my wife at home and wished she were with me.

I decided I'd better go to bed before I got all sentimental and weepy. I downed the last of my wine with a toast to Henrik and Ron somewhere on the Camino and went to my room. I'd like to think I slept that night the sleep of a partially deserving pilgrim.

6

GIFTS

*There are no days in life so memorable
as those which vibrate to some stroke
of the imagination.*

—RALPH WALDO EMERSON,
THE CONDUCT OF LIFE

I woke to the sound of horns and cymbals and thumping drums. By coincidence I'd arrived in Astorga on the eve of Santa Semana, Holy Week. Bands were forming in the Plaza de Eduardo Castro below my window for a Palm Sunday procession. It seemed a good omen, and I decided to join the ceremony and give myself a day of rest. I showered and dressed and went downstairs for breakfast in the dining room. I felt very content to linger over my café con leche by the window and watch the preparations for the festivities.

After breakfast, I joined the crowd in front of the Cathedral of Astorga and followed the procession as it slowly wound its way along the narrow streets. It was a crisp and sunny day, warm in the sun and chilly in the shadows of the buildings. I stopped like everyone else for the prayers and speeches as the procession halted in front of churches along the route. I couldn't follow the words very well, but I was happy to tag along. I admired the priests in their brocaded robes, the women in glossy fur coats, and the children in ankle-length gowns and tall cone hats, their faces hidden behind cowls that left only their eyes visible. While the older and bigger boys shouldered the elaborately decorated platforms holding brightly painted statues of the Virgin or Christ riding a donkey to the gates of Jerusalem, the younger children walked beside or in front of them waving palm fronds. People lined each side of the street, and as the procession advanced they would join the throng until there must have been a couple thousand people strolling along Calle de Villafranca back to the plaza in front of the cathedral where the ceremony ended.

When the crowd dispersed I visited the Museo de los Caminos in the neo-Gothic Bishop's Palace across from my hotel. I didn't stay long. The displays on the history of the Santiago pilgrimage were interesting enough, but I felt restless and almost claustrophobic. My body, it seemed, wanted to be moving. So I left and explored the streets until my restlessness dissipated. I was pleased to realize there was no pain in my legs or feet beyond some soreness at the back of my heels. When I'd tired myself out, I found a bar in La Peseta Hotel in the Plaza de San Bartolomé and sat at a table by the window to catch up on my pilgrimage notes, write a few postcards, and with another café con leche eat a few *mantecados*, the sticky almond pastry for which Astorga is famous. By the time I finished my notes and cards it was late afternoon. I meandered back to the hotel to have a couple of drinks, another leisurely dinner, and an early night.

I was up the next morning and on the road before 7 a.m. An overnight rain had left the air smelling sweet. I followed the Camino as it climbed up and down across the mist-shrouded valleys of the Maragatería, the chill of the mountain air giving the walk an invigorating edge. It was good to be back on the road.

Ahead of me in the distance I saw the Montes de León, the snowy peaks shining white in the sun. This was the country of the Maragatos. A people distinct from other Spaniards, the Maragatos have lived in the region between Astorga and Ponferrada to the west for well over a thousand years. Some scholars claim they are descended from Christian Visigoths or Celts, while others trace them to eighth-century Moors or Berbers from Morocco. Another theory links them to the Christian Mozarabs who lived in southern Spain among the Moors before the *Reconquista*. Yet after the discovery of a Punic necropolis in a Maragato village in the 1950s, some researchers have concluded the Maragatos were the descendants of Phoenician sailors and Iberians enslaved by the Romans to work in the region's gold mines. Whatever their origins, the Maragatos were famous during the Middle Ages as muleteers and carriers, hauling goods over the mountains and valleys between

Castile and Galicia.[1] It was once common to see Maragatos in their traditional costumes: the men wearing large slouched hats and broad-bottomed breeches called *zaragüelles* with red garters, and the women in crescent-shaped caps covered by mantles, wearing heavy black skirts and fancy filigree earrings. Apparently, after centuries of isolation, only a few thousand true Maragatos remained. Supposedly, you can recognize a Maragato woman by her fondness for "lime-green stretch slacks and horn-rimmed glasses."[2]

I kept an eye out for women in slacks, lime-green or otherwise, as I traipsed through Murias de Rechivaldo and Santa Catalina de Somoza, but saw no one. Both villages seemed deserted. The narrow streets were empty and the windows shuttered. El Ganso, too, was a derelict hamlet of crumbling walls and buckled slate roofs. Even the Cowboy Bar my guidebook referred to seemed abandoned, its doors and windows missing. The road through the village was a rutted mixture of mud, straw, and cow manure. I stepped carefully. If it hadn't been for the utility wires and the occasional car, I could have been walking through a medieval village that had somehow survived into the modern world. It was almost spooky.[3]

Actually, I walked through El Ganso with caution. One pilgrim book I'd read warned that the village dogs were particularly nasty. With my Hillmaster at the ready, and my knife accessible this time, I stepped like a nervous gunfighter, ears pricked for the sound of growling dogs. Only it wasn't growling I heard. It was the clucking of chickens. Rounding a corner on a muddy street, I found myself face to beak with a flock of them, maybe twenty or more, in the middle of the road, effectively blocking my passage. They made quite a cackle as I approached. I stopped. How do you behave around chickens? I hadn't been in a barnyard since I was a boy, when I fell into the pigpen on my Great-Uncle Edward's farm while wearing my Sunday best suit. Should I just wander nonchalantly into their midst, assuming they'd get out of the way? Would a Maragato housewife in lime-green stretch slacks come running out of her house with a carving knife if I upset her egg-laying hens? I plucked up my courage and slowly moved forward, carefully swinging my walking stick back and forth to clear a path. I didn't want to ruffle any feathers. But I did.

Suddenly there was a loud and angry squawk that startled me. I spun around to confront my attacker: a cocksure red rooster—quite a big one—giving me a mean and low look. He charged, and I beat a hasty retreat, stumbling backward so fast among the now-hysterical hens that I almost tripped and fell in the mud. Luckily I had stumbled into a wall, which allowed me to sidle along the length of the street without fear of falling while fending off the rooster with my stick and shouting rude things at him and his flock. After about two or three minutes of this nonsense the rooster finally decided I was no longer trying to lay claim to his brood. He let me go with a raucous warning and strutted back to the clearly impressed hens. While they clucked and clustered around him, I scuttled away, my boots and the legs of my pants smeared with chicken crap and feathers.

I stopped for lunch a few kilometers down the road, sitting against a crumbling, weed-laced stone wall to eat bread and cheese and the remains of a *mantecado*. Afterward, I tried to clean myself up, plucking feathers off my boots and pants. It was pleasant to sit out of the wind with the sun warm on my face. As I gazed around my bucolic bower I spotted a flash of color on the ground beside the tree trunk: four neatly quartered sections of orange peel, the edges curled and the rind dark. So here he was again, my phantom friend the Orange-Peel Man. I laughed, imagining that he had also encountered the chickens and had retreated to this wall to console himself with an orange. Seeing those neatly sliced rinds again gave me a sense of comfort. At that moment, I realized that after nearly three weeks on the Camino I was strangely content. And for a few moments there was no place else that I wanted to be other than where I was: sitting against the wall, with my legs stretched out on the grass, staring at the branches of the oak tree swaying in the wind. Of course the moment didn't last long. I soon packed away my food, got to my feet, hoisted my pack, and cast a final grateful glance at the orange peels as I returned to the road.

An hour later, just as it started to rain, I walked into Rabanal del Camino. Rabanal was the ninth stop on the pilgrim route in Picaud's *Codex Calixtinus*. During the Middle Ages, it was a thriving town with a garrison of Knights Templar on duty to protect pilgrims. Today Rabanal is a tiny village with a few bars, a church, a fountain, and a scattering of stone-and-slate houses that stretch along a couple of steep and narrow streets. But it also has one of the best refugios on the Camino, the

Refugio Gaucelmo, named after a twelfth-century monk who devoted himself to helping pilgrims. The London-based Confraternity of St. James had taken over the building, next to the Church of Santa María, in 1991. They turned what was a nearly ruined house into a lovely walled enclave with a patio, a barn, a *huerta* or garden, a warm bunk room where pilgrims could enjoy hot showers, a communal room with a fireplace, and a modest library, and in the morning they served a breakfast of toast, jam, and coffee prepared by the resident *hospitaleros.*

The *hospitaleros* that month were an American brother-and-sister team, Anthony and Sherri Rosevear, whom I joined for a drink in the Mesón El Refugio while they were having lunch. Anthony was a Dominican priest from Oakland. Sherri was a retired art teacher from Denver. I guessed them to be in their early fifties. Volunteers constitute the staff of most of the refugios along the Camino, maintaining the buildings and providing advice and assistance to pilgrims. Most of those I'd met so far were Spanish or occasionally French or German. The majority of these volunteers are former pilgrims who, after walking or cycling the Camino, offer their services. Anthony and Sherri were a little different—they had yet to walk the Camino. After they'd contacted the Confraternity in London for information about the Camino, the organization asked them to serve as *hospitaleros* before making their own pilgrimage. "We've had a wonderful time this last month," Anthony said. "We've seen the whole world go through Rabanal. We've had pilgrims from all over the world."

There were a dozen or so other pilgrims in the bar that day, and they all seemed in good spirits. I heard no grousing about the weather or inadequate showers. Nobody seemed to be limping or suffering from blisters. It occurred to me that we were now veterans of the Camino, having put the blisters and the aches and pains behind us. This assessment would prove premature, at least in my case, but just then it seemed feasible.

For dinner that night I joined a group of fellow pilgrims at the Mesón El Refugio. We took a table at the back of the restaurant. There were two young Frenchmen, Patrice and Michel; an older French woman by the name of Fanny, whom I guessed to be in her fifties; a couple of middle-aged Spanish women from Barcelona, who kept to themselves; and Tara Lynn Dary, a twenty-seven-year-old from Wisconsin. Tara

Lynn was a student at the university in Bilbao and was spending her spring break walking the Camino between Astorga and Santiago. Our collective conversation was a babble of French, Spanish, and English. Maybe it was the wine, but despite the language barriers we managed to understand each other enough to laugh at or commiserate about our adventures. My encounter with the chickens of El Ganso got a laugh. Patrice and Michel had us in hysterics as they described stopping at a village fountain and finding themselves suddenly surrounded by a herd of sheep that butted them out of the way to get to the water, leaving them covered in mud and smelling of sheep dung.

Listening to the pilgrim stories, I was again conscious of how much I was enjoying myself: the food, the wine, my companions, and even the commercial hospitality of Antonio Pérez, the restaurant owner, who was dressed as a proper waiter in tie and vest and kept bringing jugs of wine that none of us had ordered. I decided that sitting in the smoky low-ceilinged bar, being warm and dry at the end of the day's walk, and having a full belly and a head full of wine was a fine way to live. I said something to that effect. Tara Lynn summed it up nicely: "You walk, you get somewhere, you eat, you drink, you sleep. What more do you want?" At that moment I couldn't think of anything.

When I returned to the refugio I found Sherri sitting with a few other pilgrims in front of the fire, talking about her reasons for wanting to walk the Camino. "At first, I thought of it as just an adventure—you know, something different to do. And the history of it. I wanted to be part of a twelve-hundred-year-old history, with my name in the pilgrim book along with all the other pilgrim names." She paused. "I still think that, but after this last month, seeing the other pilgrims, my reasons have changed. I guess it's more religious now."

A Belgian couple had stayed at the refugio one night the previous week, Sherri continued. They'd walked from Roncesvalles with their four-year-old son, pushing the boy in a carriage when he didn't want to walk. They'd been on the road for a month. Their younger child, a two-year-old girl, had died the previous year. "Walking the Camino was their way of grieving for their daughter," she said. "When I saw them I realized the Camino was more than just an adventure."

It rained hard in the night and was still drizzling when I left Rabanal in the morning, walking in mist and clouds through the mountains. By the time I reached Foncebadón the rain had turned to sleet. In the twelfth century, the village had a church, a hospital, and a hospice for pilgrims. Now there were only the ruins of corrals and pens and a clutch of gloomy half-collapsed houses. The steeply gabled slate roofs sprouted grass and weeds. A saying about the place among pilgrims seemed appropriate: "Who hasn't passed by way of Foncebadón doesn't know solitude or sadness."

I'd had plenty of solitude in recent days, but I felt oddly cheerful despite the lousy weather. After nearly three weeks on the Camino I was free of blisters and leg pains. By the end of each day, of course, I was weary and sometimes limping from the strain on my tendons. But by the next morning I was ready and willing to walk again. Maybe, I told myself, I'd finally learned just to walk.

This day was no exception. I put one foot in front of the other unthinkingly, just walking, attending to the heather and wild thyme and broom clinging to the rocky slopes like multicolored swatches of paint on a palette. I thought of something the twentieth-century mystic Krishnamurti once said: he was happiest when he could walk without being conscious of a single thought in his head. I hadn't attained such an inner state, but I had an inkling of what he meant. I was also aware of the sleet in my face, my soaked pants, and the cold wet stream that somehow seeped inside the hood of my rain jacket and dribbled down my back. I tried to tell myself it was only water. "Sigue caminando," as Gerard might say. Keep walking.

It was in this half-cheerful yet stoic frame of mind that I climbed Monte Irago to Cruz de Ferro. This four-foot iron cross is a famous landmark on the Camino. It sits on top of a twenty-foot wooden pole that protrudes from a huge cairn of stones. Pilgrims are supposed to add to the pile a stone from home, maintaining a tradition that dates back hundreds of years. According to legend, Gaucelmo, the twelfth-century monk devoted to serving pilgrims, erected the first cross on the pile of stones. But the cairn itself may well be traced even further back. The Romans used piles of stones to mark boundaries. Even then, passers-by liked to toss their own stones onto the mound.[4]

Near this man-made hill is a small hermitage that offers shelter. I dropped my backpack against one wall and took out of a side pocket the black stone from my son's rock collection that I'd carried for the last five hundred kilometers. I climbed a slight incline to the edge of the snow-covered cairn and looked up the steep slope to the cross at the top. I couldn't help but imagine Christ at Calvary. And I pictured the hundreds of thousands of pilgrims who'd stopped and added their stones to the pile. Now it was my turn. I brought my right arm back as far as I could and threw my son's stone to the top of the pile. I saw it hit about two-thirds of the way up the slope, bounce once, twice, three times, until it disappeared in the mass of rock. A prayer seemed appropriate, but what came to mind were some half-remembered lines from one of R. S. Thomas's poems about "my boy" being tall and fair and young yet, and the line "Keep his feet free of the world's net."[5]

I walked back to the hermitage, strapped on my pack, and trundled down the road. The Camino curved along the edge of the mountain, overlooking the Valle del Silencio, the Valley of Silence. The sleet had eased, and I enjoyed a wide-angle view of the landscape below, of Mount Teleno in the distance, and of the gray outline of the mountains of Galicia on the horizon. Monks had come to this isolated region as early as the sixth century, fleeing not only the predations of the barbarians that had descended on the Roman Empire, but also the unwanted diversions of the world. Many lived as hermits, searching for God in their solitude. As I walked while scanning the valley below, I imagined another self, a double who would turn off the road and follow a path down the mountain where he would find some old hermit's hut and live there until the required conversion took place, if possible. The image brought me to a halt at a bend in the road. I found myself actually looking for a path that might lead down the slope, envisioning my other self disappearing into the trees below. Shaking off the vision, I turned back to the road in front of me and resumed my walk.

Early in the afternoon I reached El Acebo, with its old stone houses and wooden balconies looming over the narrow streets. I found a bar where a dozen or so pilgrims were sheltering from the weather. I recognized Fanny and Patrice and Michel, whom I'd dined with in Rabanal. There was a big wood-burning cast-iron stove surrounded by chairs draped with wet pants and socks and shirts, all steaming in the heat and emitting a pungent odor. I was soaked, too, so I went to the washroom to exchange my wet clothes for drier ones and then found some space for my soggy garments on a chair near the stove. I sat on a barstool next to Fanny and ordered a ham *bocadillo,* a café con leche, and a snifter of cognac.

Among the many things I enjoyed about Spain were the bartenders—not only their dignified politeness but also their generosity. In many North American bars I would have been served only a jigger-splash of bar stock barely deep enough for a fly to dangle its legs in. Spanish bartenders, however, don't use jiggers. I watched in fascination as the bartender set a great goblet on the bar and filled it halfway to the brim with Courvoisier. My monster drink, the café con leche in a large bowl, and the thick ham-and-cheese sandwich cost 400 pesetas, or about $4. Spain, I thought, might be a good place for retirement.

I spent an hour at the bar in El Acebo, warming my hands around the bowl of coffee and reheating my blood with the cognac. Other pilgrims arrived—including the American woman, Tara Lynn Dary—and they added their damp clothes to the ring of garments near the stove. In short order we had a pilgrim party going, with bottles of wine passing back and forth around the bar. The rain and sleet provided a good excuse, but eventually somebody reclaimed their pilgrim discipline and headed out the door. That prompted the rest of us to get moving, too. We repacked our damp clothes, shouldered our packs, and laughingly trooped outside only to discover that while we'd been partying, the rain had let up and the sun had come out. For some reason, that produced even more laughter.

Tara Lynn and I walked together toward Molinaseca, following the Camino as it wound along the edges of steep slopes dotted with oaks and poplars coming into leaf. Clumps of cistus with small red or yellow flowers and drifts of ivory broom carpeted the hillsides. We ambled through groves of chestnut trees. The air was filled with a cinnamon-like smell that reminded me of incense. It was like walking through an open-air church.

By late afternoon we strolled through the Puerta de los Peregrinos and over the Río Meruelo, following the main road into the pretty town of Molinaseca. The refugio was in a former church on the Ponferrada Road on the west side of town. Logs were ablaze in the ground-floor fireplace. Only one other pilgrim was there—a dark-haired Spanish woman who introduced herself as Eva Lerin. After the daily ritual of showering, hanging up wet clothes, and cleaning boots, we sat with Javier, the resident *hospitalero*. He stamped the *credenciales* and offered each of us a glass of wine.

I flipped through the refugio registration book, reading the comments of other pilgrims. Most of them addressed the trials and the joys of the Camino. Everybody, it seemed, was grateful for having walked as far as they had. I found an entry by Shirley MacLaine: "Baby, you are almost there. Each step, each day brings you closer to yourself." It wasn't the most profound thought, but then I didn't have any to offer, either. It had been a good day's walking. What more was there to say?

After the wine, the three of us—Tara Lynn, Eva, and I—walked back into Molinaseca to have dinner at the Mesón El Palacio. It was a lovely dining room: all black beams and white walls and with a large brass-plated, pyramid-shaped fireplace in the center of the room. During our meal the two women gave me a lesson in how Spain had slowly become more liberal and democratic after Franco's death in 1975. I told them about my having hitchhiked through Spain that same year and how everything looked poor and run-down and how surprised I was now to see construction projects and roadwork in even the smallest villages. Spain, they told me, was booming thanks in large part to its membership in the European Union. Eva said that while prosperity was changing Spanish society—"everybody wants a car and a cell phone"—and the influence of the Church wasn't as strong as it used to be, much of the traditional way of life remained, particularly the strong ties of family across the generations.

I thought back to my evening promenade in Pamplona and how I'd been surprised to see teenagers walking arm-in-arm with their parents or grandparents. And I recalled how often I'd seen children in bars, playing or even sitting quietly at the tables while the adults drank and talked. I asked Eva about that. "Children are the center of Spanish life," she said, explaining that Spanish parents take their children everywhere, but they don't need to be amused and pacified with entertainment. Children were taught to conduct themselves properly in social settings. That perhaps explained why the Spanish children I'd encountered were so polite and respectful. I wondered how long that tradition would last.

I gained a glimpse of this attitude toward children the next day when I walked by myself through Ponferrada, an industrial town at the conflu-ence of the Boeza and Sil rivers where the Camino enters the Bierzo valley. I had reached the town late in the morning. The yellow arrows took me across the Puente Mascarón and along Bajada de San Andrés and Calle del Temple beneath the massive ramparts of a medieval castle built by the Knights Templar to fend off the Moors. Twice I lost my way in the maze of streets. Each time, someone—an elderly man on one oc-casion, a middle-aged woman on the other—came out of a shop to point me in the right direction. The woman, chattering in Spanish, planted a kiss on both my cheeks before laughingly sending me on my way.

But even with help I had trouble finding the route through the city back to the Camino. I decided to take a break and stopped at a small corner bar on the tree-lined Avenida de las Huertas del Sacramento to have my morning café con leche and churro and to study my map. I was the only customer except for three women enjoying their morning *café corto*. I sat at a table by the window. The woman who ran the place took my order, but her daughter, a little girl about eight years old with long shiny black hair and big brown eyes, placed the coffee and pastry in front of me.

"Muchas gracias, señorita," I said, smiling. Maybe it was my appall-ing accent, but she giggled and backed away. Her mother said something I couldn't catch, and the child stopped laughing and became serious.

"De nada, señor," she said, acknowledging my thanks with a slight nod of her head. The shy giggles, however, returned, and she ran back to her mother behind the bar.

It didn't take long to plot my route out of Ponferrada, but I stayed for about an hour, enjoying the quiet, catching up on my notes, watching the cars pass on the boulevard, and grinning at the little girl when she dared to poke her head around the corner of the bar. I figured I'd prob-ably strayed off the Camino route through the city and she didn't usu-ally see many pilgrims; maybe my mud-stained clothes and unshaven face gave me a certain exotic appeal. I ordered another coffee just to see if she'd break into giggles again. Somehow, though, she contained herself and carried the big bowl to my table with a charming solemnity.

Finally, though, it was time to leave. I asked the girl's mother for the bill, and she gave it to the girl to bring to me on a small white saucer. I placed the money on the saucer and handed it back to the child. I asked her name. "¿Qué es tu nombre, señorita?" She was too shy to speak, but from behind the bar her mother answered, "Chonina."

I explained as best I could that I was a pilgrim walking to Santiago de Compostela—"Soy un peregrino que va a Santiago"—as if they couldn't tell. On impulse, I pulled my scallop shell from a side pocket of my pack. I remembered wondering whether I'd ever earn it or feel like a real pilgrim. In my stumbling, inadequate Spanish I said I wanted to give the shell to Chonina. The child looked at her mother, who nodded her approval. I handed it to the girl and watched as she rubbed her small fingers on its pearly smooth inside. I didn't have the words to explain what the shell represented, but her mother said something to her. I caught the words *peregrino* and Santiago.

Chonina and her mother followed me outside as I left the restaurant. The woman spoke to her daughter and urged her forward. Chonina held out her hand. "Gracias, señor, por la concha."

"Usted es bienvenido, Chonina," I said, hoping I was saying "you're welcome" correctly. We shook hands. She was going to have long fingers when she grew up, I thought, and she'll be a beauty.

I shook hands with Chonina's mother, too. As I turned away, she touched my arm and said, "Por favor, señor, un abrazo por el apóstol." She was referring to the tradition of pilgrims hugging the statue of St. James in the cathedral at Santiago.

I was touched and flattered. It's a serious matter for someone to ask you to remember him or her to St. James. It meant the woman regarded me as a serious pilgrim and expected me to act accordingly. "Sí." I will remember. Walking away, I glanced back to see Chonina's mother crossing herself. It gave me a good feeling.

That feeling stayed with me all day as I walked across the rolling green hills of El Bierzo with its vineyards, orchards, and tobacco fields. The smell of spring saturated the air, and I often stopped simply to breathe in deeply as though I could absorb the fields and the hills into my body. Sometimes I stopped just to listen to the water splashing over the stones of the small creeks that ran alongside the pilgrim route. At other times the Camino was little more than a path hemmed in by trees and shrubs.

I reached Villafranca del Bierzo, one of the loveliest towns on the Camino, late in the afternoon. Established in the eleventh century by French immigrants, the town once had eight monasteries and six pilgrim hospitals. One of the surviving churches, the Romanesque Church of Santiago, still has a *puerta del perdón*—a doorway of forgiveness—that those pilgrims too weary or ill to continue need only touch to receive the same indulgences they'd have received if they'd been able to reach Santiago.[6] Judging by the large cemetery adjacent to the church, many pilgrims didn't make it beyond Villafranca del Bierzo. Those who did go further, as I did, descended from the church along the cobblestone Calle del Agua, passing homes with stone coats of arms on the walls and wrought-iron balconies cluttered with flower pots. I checked into the local public refugio, getting a bunk across from a Spanish family. That night for supper I went to a private refugio run by one of Villafranca's better-known residents, at least among pilgrims: Jesús Arias Jato.

A muscular man with a salt-and-pepper beard and gray hair, Jato was a local farmer and entrepreneur until he had a heart attack many years ago and nearly died. The near-death experience—Jato actually claims he did die and was revived—inspired him. After he recovered, Jato and his family began providing food and shelter to the pilgrims passing through town. When I was there, his refugio on Avenida Fenix, down the road from the Church of Santiago, was little more than a couple of Quonset-like structures covered in plastic sheeting. You could get a meal of *caldo gallego*, the regional soup, along with a platter of beef and vegetables, baskets of bread, and all the red wine you could drink for about ten dollars.

But Jato's real claim to fame among pilgrims was his Ritual of the Burning, a nightly ceremony that gained him a reputation as something of a shaman. I don't know if anyone took the ritual seriously, but it was fun to watch. Adopting the theatrical mannerisms of a New York bartender, Jato poured long streams of various kinds of alcohol into a metal tureen. He then took a lighter and, standing back a safe distance, set the contents ablaze. That's when the lights went out. In the darkness Jato started a patter of chants and incantations as he dipped a ladle into the flaming tureen, pulled out a stream of burning liquid, and then poured it—still burning—into a line of mismatched cups and glasses. Each pilgrim received a share. Jato intoned some sort of benediction, raised his cup, and dumped it down his throat, gesturing for the pilgrims to do likewise. Some did. The more cautious ones, myself included, blew out the flame and sipped carefully.[7]

Sometimes, I'd heard, Jato repeated the ceremony, depending on the number of pilgrims present. I didn't stay to find out. Despite my good mood I was apprehensive about the next day's walk. My guidebook described the thirty-kilometer climb to the mountain village of O Cebreiro in Galicia as long, steep, and strenuous.

7

VISIONS

*I know well what I am fleeing from
but not what I am in search of.*
—MICHEL DE MONTAIGNE,
ESSAYS

I strained to see through the fog, trying to spot a yellow arrow or a splotch of paint to convince myself I wasn't lost. I'd been walking for nearly four hours since leaving Villafranca del Bierzo early that morning, following the Camino route to Trabadelo and Vega de Valcárce. It had rained hard most of the way, but now, only a dismal drizzle.

The route follows the Río Valcárce as it cascades down a steep-sided, wooded valley that cuts through the last set of mountains before Galicia. It might have been a pleasant walk if not for the rain and the stream of cars and trucks spewing diesel fumes and road spray as they roared by. In Portela, I rested by the river beneath the oak trees and ate an orange while watching the trout rise in the eddies along the bank. Later that morning, nauseated by the fumes I'd been inhaling and slightly deafened by the traffic, I stopped for my café con leche at a roadside hotel outside Vega de Valcárce. I studied my maps, mentally preparing myself for the long climb to O Cebreiro. I'd walked about twenty kilometers and had another dozen or so to go.

Two hours later, I wondered if I'd taken the right route. The road from Vega de Valcárce to Herrerias was a gentle climb, and I made good time despite the rain. But beyond Herrerias the footpath climbed steeply, zigzagging upward through chestnut woods to the village of La Faba. By the time I reached Laguna de Castilla, about three kilometers beyond La Faba, I was running out of energy. To make the situation worse, I was climbing in a bank of cloud so thick I sometimes couldn't see more than a few yards in front of me or on either side of the trail. I knew I had roughly another eight or nine kilometers of hard climbing before I reached O Cebreiro. But walking in the cloudy mist left me disoriented and fearful that I'd inadvertently wandered onto a path leading away from the pilgrimage route. I had no idea how far I'd come since I couldn't see where I'd been, and I couldn't estimate how far I had to go since I couldn't see much of anything ahead. And except for the squelching of my boots on the muddy path, the patter of rain on my jacket and hat, and my own labored breathing, I heard nothing at all.

Rationally, I knew there was no way I could get lost so long as I stayed on the path. I knew the law of gravity would keep me on the ground. I knew I was climbing since I could feel the forward tilt of my body and the strain in my legs. Every now and then a copse of wind-twisted scrub oak loomed out of the fog, and I felt connected to reality. But at other times it seemed the entire world—trees, rocks, flowers, fields, sky—had disappeared behind a veil of gauze, leaving me alone in some cloud of unknowing with only my thoughts to convince me I was still in the world.

I took comfort from my walking stick. Gripping it, seeing it stab into the mud, and leaning on it to ease the strain in my legs provided a physical reminder that there was more to being in the world than thinking. Yet when I stood still, surrounded by fog and silence, it was easy to imagine myself as a disembodied consciousness floating in some opaque and formless space. Like the fog curling around the trees and boulders, tendrils of crazy thoughts twisted through my mind. Was this what it was like to cross the borderland of consciousness into death? Did the mind just drift away from the body? Did your consciousness fold inward like a collapsing star, getting smaller and smaller until the brief brightness that was your life—all those memories, ideas, and dreams—blinked out, disappearing into the immense unknown from which you came?

Such speculations kept me company as I staggered wet and weary along the narrow path. I thought of returning to Vega de Valcárce, where presumably I could find a taxi, but I couldn't be sure that wouldn't lead me astray. There was nothing to do but keep walking. And so I did, until I lost all sense of time and direction and, as it sometimes seemed, self-awareness.

Occasionally I snapped back to myself, startled to realize that I couldn't remember what I'd seen—not that there was much to see in the fog—or what I'd been thinking, if anything, for the previous five or ten minutes. Taking a drink from my water bottle, chewing a piece of bread, whacking a stone with my walking stick—such physical acts reminded me I was still a solid, separate entity confronting the world. Even so, I was increasingly desperate for the comfort of a yellow arrow, something to tell me that I wasn't alone and that I was heading in the right direction.

I should have had more faith in the Camino. As I plodded along a zigzagging section of the trail, my nose detected the cloying smell of a barnyard. I followed the scent until I heard the clonking of cowbells. The path swung sharply into a *corredoira*, one of the myriad narrow paths bordered by stone walls that local farmers use to herd their cows and sheep. On my right, I saw the vague shape of a stone barn and cows behind a dilapidated fence.

I kept walking, with my head lowered against the drizzling rain. The sound of cowbells faded, but relief was at hand. One moment I was tromping on a strip of pebbly earth, and the next I was walking across flat, rain-slick asphalt. The sudden change in the texture of the path startled me so much that I almost tripped over my own feet. I looked around. Ahead of me on the sloping road, barely visible in the fog, were a couple of *pallozas*, circular rough stone dwellings with conical thatched roofs; these were the famous houses of O Cebreiro, whose design dates to the Celtic era.

The village is little more than a cluster of a dozen or so *pallozas* on a weather-lashed plateau in the Sierra de Ancares mountains. On the west side of the mountains is Galicia, Spain's hinterland—a green, misty, and remote region with a history dating to the Celtic invasions of 1000 BC. Centuries later, Roman soldiers built a fort on the plateau that allowed them to see the approach of enemies from miles away. In the tenth century, long after the Romans had departed, Carthusian monks recolonized the aerie, building a monastery on the ruins of a pagan temple.[1]

I peered through the mist that shrouded the tiny village to make sure I wasn't hallucinating. I remembered something Nancy Frey had written about O Cebreiro—that it's a place where, after the hard climb, pilgrims become susceptible to visions.[2] Maybe others were susceptible in that way, but just then I wasn't feeling particularly visionary. I trembled with exhaustion. My leg muscles, suddenly relaxing after the climb, twitched and cramped. I was soaking wet and felt chilled. The only vision I had was of a warm room, a hot shower, and a bottle of wine. I staggered the last couple hundred yards on that nice flat asphalt road to the Hostal San Giraldo de Aurillac.

My vision of comfort soon faded. The small hotel was fully booked, which I should have known from the sight of the Mercedes, Audis, and BMWs crammed into the parking lot. The restaurant, too, was packed. I couldn't even get a coffee. O Cebreiro is a national Spanish monument, and the *pallozas*—where locals once lived with their cows, pigs, and donkeys—had become a tourist attraction. It looked as though I would have to stay in the refugio on the edge of the village, even though I had no desire to spend the night in what I assumed would be a crowded bunkroom and, more to the point, surrounded by people. My other option was traipsing an additional three or four kilometers to Linares, where I might be able to get a room for the night. Only I didn't want to walk anymore. I trundled around the village looking for another café where I could get warm before deciding what to do.

The Camino gods—Celtic or Christian—decided for me. As I came around the corner of a *palloza*, a short, dark-haired woman in black emerged from the door of a low-walled building and gestured for me to approach.

"Ven aquí, ven aquí. ¿Necesita una habitación?"

I sure did need a room. Did she have any vacancies? "¿Tienen ustedes habitaciónes libres?" I tried to ask.

"Sí. Sí. Aquí."

"¿Ducha de agua caliente?" I was desperate for a hot shower.

"Sí, con ducha," she answered, waving me toward the open door behind her.

And so I found a lovely warm room in the home of Esperanza Nuñez Pérez. Her four-room *pensión* provided me with the most luxurious accommodations I would enjoy on the Camino outside a high-end hotel. She led me down a short hallway that opened onto a parlor with three couches in a semicircle facing a huge stone fireplace. A roaring fire warmed the room. Half a dozen nicely dressed young women were sitting there, surrounded by babies and toddlers. Diaper bags, toys, blankets, and bottles of wine covered the low table in front of the couches. Babies were crying and women laughing. Two of the women were breastfeeding as I walked into the room. They glanced my way and without missing a beat in their conversation calmly covered themselves with shawls. I followed Señora Pérez down another hallway to a door on the right. She stepped aside to let me look inside.

"Bella," I said. Beautiful. And it was. The walls were of thick gray stone and dark wood beams, with a white ceiling divided by more beams. In the middle of the room was a queen-sized canopy bed covered in a brightly colored quilt. Fat pillows in red covers were propped against the dark headboard. Brass lamps with red shades sat on the small bedside tables. It looked warm, cozy, and inviting. Best of all— and Señora Pérez seemed proud to show it—was a gleaming bathroom with porcelain and chrome-plated fixtures and fluffy white towels. I was a little stunned. I felt like a bear that had stumbled into the perfect den for winter hibernation. "Bella," I said again.

Smiling at my obvious pleasure, Señora Pérez took my passport to record in the *pensión* register and my *credencial* to stamp and left me to my own devices. I dumped my pack in the corner, quickly shed my soggy clothes and messy boots, and climbed into the shower. I let the hot water run until the shivers were gone. My aching muscles sighed in relief. When I emerged half an hour later I found my passport and *credencial* on one of the bedside tables, along with a big bowl of café con leche. How did she know what I wanted? Señora Pérez, I vowed, would get a prayer from me in Santiago. Wrapped in a towel, I sat on the bed, propped myself up against the pillows, and sipped the steaming coffee. When the bowl was empty I stretched out, pulled the quilt over my legs, and fell asleep, a contented pilgrim.

The laughter of women pulled me from my slumbers. I didn't mind. I lay in the dim light of the room, warm beneath the quilt, listening to the rise and fall of their voices. They were definitely getting louder as the evening progressed. I got up, dressed, and after spreading my wet clothes on the radiator, headed out to find food. Except for some bread and cheese and a couple of oranges, I hadn't had anything to eat since the morning. As I walked through the parlor, I couldn't help but notice a pretty young woman with shoulder-length auburn hair on one of the couches facing the hallway. She was nursing a baby, her breasts exposed. She looked up at me as I walked by and smiled, making no effort to cover herself. Maybe I should have looked away out of politeness, but she really had lovely breasts. As I closed the door behind me, the women burst into laughter again. That made me smile.

The heart of O Cebreiro is the pre-Romanesque Church of Santa María la Real, parts of which date to the ninth century. Inside the church, a statue of a round-faced Virgin holding the Christ child in her lap greeted me. I kept thinking of the auburn-haired woman with the baby at her breast in the *pensión*.

The church's most famous artifact is a chalice displayed in an illuminated, bulletproof case. Legend identifies the gold-and-blue enameled chalice with the Holy Grail. In the late thirteenth century, according to the legend, an old priest, irritated at having to celebrate Mass for one lone shepherd, derided the man's faith even though the shepherd had struggled through a nasty storm to get to Mass. But as the priest carped and complained through the moments of the Transfiguration, both he and the shepherd were startled—and no doubt terrified—to see the host and the wine transformed into flesh and blood.[3]

It was still light when I left the church. The rain had let up sufficiently for me to walk around the village without getting drenched. Even the ubiquitous fog had lifted. At the western edge of O Cebreiro I had a panoramic view of quilt-patterned farm fields, crisscrossing roads, hedgerows, and small clusters of buildings in the valley below. As I gazed at the landscape, I remembered some of the region's history. During the Peninsular War against the French, the British Army suffered one of its blackest days in this area. In 1809, hundreds of British soldiers, along with women and children camp followers, froze to death here as they fled Marshal Soult's troops pursuing them from Villafranca. In the chaos, the army's paymasters backed the wagons to the edge of the cliffs and heaved bags of gold coins over the mountainside in an attempt to lighten the load. The gold was supposed to be used to pay the soldiers. Because they had no food for their horses, and in order to conserve ammunition, the soldiers herded the starving animals to the edge of the plateau and forced them over the precipice.[4] Staring at the bright emerald and lime-green canvas below me, I couldn't help but imagine the screaming horses and the whimpering men, women, and children as they lay in the roadside ditches waiting for death.

I turned away from my imaginings and walked back to the village in search of food, including some bread and cheese for the next day. Señora Pérez directed me to a low-ceiled tavern in a palazzo across the street from her *pensión*. I had an empanada—a pie filled with meat and soft white cheese and honey—and a bottle of *vino tinto*. Sitting there after the meal and slowly draining the bottle, I enjoyed the smoky warmth of the place and caught up on my notes. When I felt sleepy I returned to my room at the *pensión*. I spent half an hour cleaning my boots and laying out my clothes for the morning and then had another shower before climbing into bed. The noise of people gathering in the parlor and the clink of glasses and bottles were oddly comforting. I fell asleep to the muffled sounds of women's laughter and the image of a woman with a child.

I awoke at 6 a.m. from a dreamless sleep. Mentally scanning my body for aches and pains, I found none except for the usual stiffness in my heels. Despite the rigors of the previous day's walk, I was ready to walk again. Admittedly, I wasn't eager to leave my warm bed and go out in the rain I heard pelting the window. But I'd learned to accept the weather. I headed for the shower.

An hour later, Señora Pérez knocked on my door to deliver the bill—3,500 pesetas, or about $35—and to tell me breakfast would be available in the parlor. I ate alone in a room that felt empty and forlorn without the women and their babies. When I had finished the coffee and bread and jam, I thanked my hostess and told her she had a beautiful home—"Usted tiene una casa hermosa"—and I was glad to have stayed. Then I went out the door and into the chill, wet morning. Glancing back, I saw Señora Pérez in the doorway, crossing herself as Chonina's mother had done when I left. I made a mental note to hug the apostle on her behalf, too, when I reached Santiago.

The highway out of O Cebreiro drops steeply and then climbs just as steeply toward Alto de Poio, one of the highest points on the Camino at 1,337 meters above sea level. I bypassed Linares, which was just off the highway in the valley below O Cebreiro, and walked through the tiny hamlet of Hospital de la Condesa without stopping. Señora Pérez's breakfast saw me through a couple of hours of walking. I took a break at the Bar Puerto in Alto de Poio, about nine kilometers from O Cebreiro. Inside was the Spanish family I'd met at the refugio in Villafranca del Bierzo: Jesús Royo and his wife, Assumpta, and Jesús's niece, Alba Arias.

"Hola, Roberto," said Jesús. "Join us."

"Hola, Jesús," I replied. Jesús, a husky, dark-haired man, was a high-school teacher in Barcelona and spoke English well. Assumpta, a slender, athletic-looking woman, worked with disabled children. They'd been walking sections of the Camino for two years. The previous year they'd walked from Roncesvalles to León. This year they were walking two hundred kilometers from León to Sarria, accompanied by twelve-year-old Alba, who was on school break. They hoped to complete the last hundred kilometers from Sarria to Santiago next year. On this morning they'd also walked from O Cebreiro, where they'd spent the night in the refugio. It hadn't been crowded or cramped at all, Jesús said. They'd had it to themselves.

I told them about my beautiful *pensión* and the laughing women. Day-trippers, Jesús explained. Spain's burgeoning middle-class has discovered sightseeing, and O Cebreiro lured them with a taste of the Camino. For many Spaniards, traveling the Camino is something they feel they must do at least once in their lives. "The Camino has been part of Spain's history for twelve hundred years," he said. "When you walk it, you are part of that history. Everywhere you go, you are surrounded by history."

Jesús paused, glancing at Assumpta and Alba. "The road you are walking has seen millions of people. You, like them, are a small thing in the movement of eternity. You will die someday, disappear like all those others." He stabbed his spoon at me. "But the Camino will still be there."

I walked with Jesús and his family to the village of Fonfría del Camino. Five hundred years earlier, there'd been a pilgrim refuge here that provided free food and shelter for both healthy and sick pilgrims.[5] Nowadays, all that remains is a scattering of ramshackle houses and an odorous cow path. Beyond Fonfría, the elevation of the Camino dropped sharply as we approached Triacastela. It was sheer pleasure to be walking downhill, especially when the rain had stopped. The land-scape changed, too. I left behind the open country of the mountains with their splashes of white broom and thickets of gorse for dense oak and chestnut groves and patches of brightly colored heather. I was in Galicia.

Aimery Picaud described this leg of the Camino as a richly endowed region with fine orchards, plentiful fruits, and clear springs, but with few towns and villages or cultivated fields.[6] Several hundred years later, it still seemed an apt description. The trail cut across terraced *mini-fundios*, or small landholdings, and wound along narrow green lanes through villages of huddling stone. The architecture was also different from elsewhere along the Camino. Houses made of differently sized stones stacked one on top of the other replaced the red pantile roofs and whitewashed walls of Castilian homes. I also saw my first gable-roofed *hórreos*, the long, rectangular granaries built of wood or stone and set on pillars to protect the grain from rodents and dampness.[7]

We stopped for lunch at the Casa de Biduedo, a restaurant in a vil-lage about two or three kilometers west of Fonfría. Jesús insisted on ordering for me: a freshly baked empanada stuffed with pork and green peppers, a small tortilla *española*, some Roquefort-like Cabrales cheese made, as he explained, from cow's and goat's milk, a fresh garden salad, and a couple of ice-cold bottles of white Ribeira wine. It made for a leisurely two-hour lunch. As we ate, we talked. I still wanted to know why Jesús was walking the Camino.

"It's not just the history, although that is important for me," he said. He paused, staring into his glass of wine. "The Camino is real. When I'm on the Camino, everything seems more real, the land and the farms and"—he laughed—"even the sheep shit."

To my own surprise, I understood what he was getting at. Until I walked the Camino, I couldn't remember another time when I'd had such a sharp awareness of nature or had felt so close to it—aware of the rocks, the flowers, and yes, the shit. Nor had I felt in such good physical shape since my youth, when naturally enough I hadn't been much aware of my body. I was certainly sleeping better than I had in years. And as I looked at the empty plates on the table, I realized I hadn't enjoyed my food so much in years, eating for sheer sensual pleasure.[8]

"Here's to the sheep of the world," I said, raising my glass in a toast.

"¡Salud! ¡Salud!" said Jesús. "Sometimes it's good to be in the shit."

We both thought that was terribly funny and started snorting and cackling. We might have kept it up and ordered another bottle of wine if Assumpta hadn't reminded us that we still had some walking to do.

"No shit," I said, which was the wrong thing to say because it started another laughing jag.

Eventually, though, we hoisted our packs and stepped out the door. Walking past a church, Jesús noticed chickens on the road and shouted, "Chicken shit." That set us off again. It set the chickens off, too. As they flapped and squawked, Jesús and I laughed so hard that we had to hang on to each other to stop from falling. Assumpta and Alba walked on ahead, trying to ignore the two *hombres borrachos* behind them.

We made it to Triacastela, where I said goodbye to Jesús and his family in front of the Mesón Vilasante on the edge of town. I planned to spend the night there, but Jesús wanted to reach Samos, another twelve kilometers down the road, and they left to find a taxi. Their departure left me deflated. I wished I'd joined them in the taxi. Despite my desire to be alone, I'd enjoyed Jesús's company.

I felt restless, and after checking in and cleaning up, I walked around town. There wasn't much to see except a few shops, a couple of banks, some bars, and a Romanesque church. But then maybe it was me and not the town. I suddenly felt depressed. It didn't help that the restaurant where I ate dinner, ordering the *menu del día*, served up an insult to Spanish cuisine: a bowl of cold *grelos* or turnip-green soup, two fried eggs that smelled a bit off, limp french fries, and a salad with tomatoes suitable for throwing in a riot. I wasn't hungry, but I ate anyway, thinking I might not eat again until the next day. As it turned out, I didn't eat much of anything for the next three days.

I was sick in the night. I awoke in the early morning hours drenched in sweat and feeling nauseated. The next thing I knew I was throwing back the sheets and racing to the bathroom, barely making it in time to vomit my dinner into the toilet. In between bouts of retching I figured it must have been the eggs I'd had for supper. The chickens were getting their revenge for my laughing at them.

Although I still felt weak and feverish by daybreak, I thought perhaps I could make it to Sarria. But I decided to play it safe. Instead of

following the Camino overland to Sarria, I decided to walk along the
road to Samos. If things got too bad I would stay in Samos or take a
taxi the last ten kilometers to Sarria. So by 8 a.m. I crossed the bridge
over the Río Oribio at San Cristobo and walked another two or three
kilometers to Renche, where I stopped for my café con leche and a sugary chocolate churro, hoping that would settle my stomach. It didn't. I
vomited in a ditch somewhere between Renche and Samos.

Feverish and trembling, I somehow made it to Samos. I don't remember much about the village beyond the impression of a clutch
of stone houses clustered around the huge seventh-century Benedictine monastery for which the town is famous. I felt lightheaded and
seemed to be seeing things from a long distance. I found a café where
the woman behind the bar was kind enough to phone for a taxi. Again,
I don't remember much about the drive to Sarria beyond the fact that
everything was very green. By noon, I'd checked into the three-star
Alfonso IX. My room cost 7,400 pesetas—about $74—a night, but
I didn't care. I wanted every technological convenience and comfort I
could get.

I spent the next two days in a splendid room with pink-and-gray
marble and terracotta tiling. There was a little refrigerator full of bottles
and a color TV I could watch from the king-sized bed. The bathroom
had a large shower-and-bath, a bidet, and a toilet with which I became
quite intimate.

When I wasn't kneeling or sitting in the bathroom, I lay in bed and
watched Spanish soap operas. I found that when I turned off the sound
I could pretty much follow the storyline. When I wasn't watching television, I curled beneath the covers in an effort to quell the shivering, or
I lay on top of them when I was drenched in sweat. I drained the juices
and bottles of water from the refrigerator, leaving the Scotch, vodka,
and wine alone. I ate nothing. The chambermaids took pity on me,
bringing fresh towels and clean sheets—for which I left them a large
tip. The front desk offered to call a doctor, but I declined. What would
a doctor prescribe that I wasn't already doing?

The fever broke on the afternoon of my second day in Sarria. The
nausea subsided, too, as did the intestinal turmoil. At first, I was angry
with myself for losing two days on the Camino. Yet the Sarria sojourn
wasn't a complete waste. I had plenty of time to reflect on my journey.

I thought about Jesús Royo's description of the Camino as more "real." Many of the pilgrims I'd met said something similar. For some of them, of course, the Camino provided a series of pleasant memories and a sense of physical accomplishment. Others, no doubt, regarded the Camino as therapy, a way to compensate for the strain and stress of their everyday lives. But surely my motives weren't that limited? Surely I hadn't put up with blisters, bad legs, smelly refugios, and food poisoning just to feel good about myself, to wallow in narcissistic wellness? Besides, I hadn't had the impression that Jesús or Henrik or Ron or Anne or Charles needed the Camino as emotional compensation. On the contrary, they seemed eminently well adjusted, perhaps more so than I. They weren't walking the Camino to escape reality but rather to engage it more deeply. Their escape, if that was the right word, was from the diversions of the world that made it so difficult to be real. What was it Henrik said? "On the Camino I have time to think about things that are important to me, things that you never have time to think about in your normal life. Like death." In this sense, I thought, the Camino was not so much therapy as a kind of space and place where you had the time and opportunity to work through existential problems.

Propped up in bed, with some orange juice at hand, I hauled my research journal out of my pack and spent the next few hours leafing through my notes and thinking about what I was supposedly doing on this pilgrimage. I found a quotation from Phil Cousineau that seemed to reflect one of the essential motives for pilgrimage: "The journeys all begin in a restive state, in deep disturbance. Something vital was missing in life: Vitality itself may be lurking on the road or at the heart of a distant sanctuary."[9] Did that apply to me? Was I restive? Was something missing from my life? Silly questions, perhaps, since most of us are missing things in our lives. We are too busy getting and spending, too caught up in career and consumption, to attend to the most necessary things. We are avoiding the existential concerns of our lives—love and death and the whole damn thing, as Woody Allen would say.

Certainly I'd looked forward to my pilgrimage as a break from the routines of daily life. It was to be an adventure that would, I hoped, lift me out of the rut of the ordinary. I knew what I didn't want anymore but not what I wanted. But the Camino had become something more than this, too. I considered another quotation from my journal: We go on pilgrimages, wrote Pico Iyer, "because every one of us carries around, inside, a certain unnamed homesickness, a longing for a place we left and don't know how to find again."[10] Maybe that's what pilgrimage is all about in the end: each of us suffers a kind of homesickness, and our journeys are a search for a home we have lost. To walk the Camino was an attempt, unconsciously or not, to address the questions for which the modern world provides little time, or which it even regards as pointless—an attempt to discover, or recover, amidst all that conspires to make us homeless, the dwelling place where the soul feels at home.

That was certainly the theme of much of the pilgrimage literature I'd read. While the television attempted to divert me with a James Bond movie—*Live and Let Die*—I continued to read through my notes, glancing up at the screen occasionally and listening to Roger Moore speaking Spanish. Every religion and culture has a tradition of pilgrimage. The Bible is in large measure a series of tales of journeys in search of meaning and purpose. Adam and Eve wandered through the wilderness searching for a new home after their expulsion from the Garden of Eden. Abraham wandered in the desert seeking the inscrutable will of Jehovah. Moses led the Israelites out of Egypt to the Promised Land. Christ suffered his temptation in the desert and struggled to understand his Father's will. Even the great works of philosophy are pilgrimage tales of sorts. In Plato's *Republic*, Socrates begins his inquiry into what constitutes a just life by walking from Athens to Piraeus to pray to the goddess. Augustine's *City of God* recounts the pilgrimage of the human soul from paganism to the worship of the one true God. Hegel's *Phenomenology of Mind* is the tale of the human spirit's historical pilgrimage from its first glimmering of awareness to full self-consciousness.[11]

I was, it seemed, in good company. Maybe going on a pilgrimage, however inchoate my motives, was the most human thing I could do. In skimming my notes, I noticed that many of the pilgrims I'd quoted were, as I was, trying to understand their motives for undertaking a pilgrimage. Edward Stanton regularly harkened to an age when, as he put it, "men and women were somehow larger than today, closer to the center, the sources of life, a mystery that has been lost to us." It took a moment of self-admonishment for him to admit the nature of the mystery to which he referred: "Shit, why don't you go ahead and say it: God."[12]

Was that my deep-seated motive, too? Sure I enjoyed the landscape, the wine and laughter, the architecture, the sense of attachment to history, and even the occasional moment of sublimity. But was my Camino ultimately a search for God? If so, why was I so reluctant to admit it? Had a lifetime in the mental corral of modernity, with its denial of all things transcendent, made it almost impossible, and indeed intellectually embarrassing, to invoke the Judeo-Christian metaphor of divine order? And if that were the case, what could I do about it? I didn't want to believe in anything if there was nothing in which to believe. But how do you know there is nothing to believe in until you try to believe? Didn't C. S. Lewis say that faith requires practice even when you don't believe?

I gave myself a break, watching Bond rescue Solitaire from the evil Dr. Kananga. But the questions wouldn't stop coming. Do you actually search for God, or does God find you? Didn't Gregory of Nyssa write, "To seek God is to find Him"?[13] What must you do in the act of seeking? How do you prepare yourself for an encounter if you aren't already sure there is something to encounter? Why bother unless you already know or, at the very least, have some glimmer of what would make the effort worthwhile? Did I seriously expect something like Paul's conversion on the road to Damascus, or the French mystic Simone Weil's experience of Christ possessing her? Was such an experience possible for me? Did I even want such an experience? Can you actually seek such moments and prepare for their possibility, or do they just happen out of the blue?

I returned to my notes to consider the notion of liminal experience that the anthropologists Victor and Edith Turner wrote about. The word comes from the Latin *limin*, meaning a doorway or threshold. According to the Turners, liminality involves moments of spiritual vision, however modest or profound, when you temporarily transcend the everyday world to experience a heightened sense of reality. Liminality, they wrote, marks a transformative period in which spiritual and psychological change can occur. In liminal experience you cross the threshold from old to new ways of perception. This, I thought, suggests that liminal moments are journeys unto themselves, pilgrimages of the psyche. To experience the Camino as a liminal event is to re-enchant the disenchanted world, to recover the extraordinary in the ordinary.[14]

Recalling particular moments during my weeks on the pilgrimage trail, it seemed to me that I'd experienced the occasional liminal event. Maybe experiences like those of St. Paul and Simone Weil were beyond me—or maybe I just wasn't ready for them—and if that were the case, I would have to be content with whatever the Camino offered. The Zen dictum came to mind again: If you sit, just sit; if you walk, just walk. That's what I had to do, too. Stop fussing and fretting about some ultimate purpose; act genuinely as a pilgrim, and let the meaning, divine or otherwise, reveal itself.

I dropped my journal on the bed and picked up my tattered copy of Eliot's *Four Quartets* from the bedside table. I read some of my favorite lines from "Little Gidding"—that what we think we come for "Is only a shell, a husk of meaning / From which the purpose breaks only when it is fulfilled / If at all."[15] But even then, as Eliot wrote, the purpose might be "altered in fulfillment." I had no idea how those lines might apply to me, but they seemed to offer worthwhile guidance. I might not understand what my pilgrimage was all about even when I reached Santiago. It might take years for a full understanding of my Camino to work itself out, if ever. As the movie credits scrolled down the screen, I turned off the TV, crawled under the covers, and fell asleep wondering what lay in store for me in the morning, hope jostling with uncertainty.

8

UNDERGLIMMER

The longest journey is the journey inward.

—DAG HAMMARSKJÖLD,
MARKINGS

As I walked out of Sarria in the morning, crossing the Río Celeiro over the Ponte Aspera, the Camino carried me into the realm of the *corredoiras* that lace the Galician countryside like threads in a tapestry. The path wound through woodlands of chestnuts and oaks, birch and pine, and here and there copses of tall, smooth-trunked eucalyptus. The trees were flush with new leaves. Shifting patterns of light and shade dappled the trail. An occasional breeze ruffled the trees, showering me with remnants of last night's rain. The air was fresh and sweet with the smell of damp earth.

I followed the path as if in a prayer labyrinth. I tried to act accordingly, moving at a meditative pace and attending to the world around me—noticing the stones and the flowers, listening to the chirping of nuthatches in the oak trees, and stopping to grant passage to the lizards and salamanders that sometimes scurried across the trail.

I felt disoriented and even a little lightheaded. My mind seemed to float above and behind my body like a balloon on a string. I walked almost without thought, aware only of the sun on my head, the wind in the trees, and the changing surface beneath my feet. My sense of detachment, of floating above it all, was no doubt due, at least in part, to my not having eaten solid food for three days. My unexpected timeout from the Camino had purged me, if not purified me. And now, it seemed, my senses wanted their fill of the world again.

This psychological shift wasn't a complete surprise to me. I'd read accounts suggesting that a pilgrim's psychic state reflects his or her physiological condition. That seemed to fit my circumstances. I felt a connection between the external experience of the Camino—the feel of mud and stone, of ruts and rivulets—and the journeys that took place in my mind. In the last three weeks of my pilgrimage I'd become more aware of the natural world—the close and constant presence of earth, air, water, and sky.[1] On foot, I was more attentive to the rhythms of nature, which in turn reinforced the quieter, calmer frame of mind encouraged by the psychology of walking.

As I responded physiologically to the terrain and the weather, I also began to reap the spiritual benefits of the Camino. My pilgrimage became as much a journey across my psychic landscape as it was a journey across northern Spain.[2] As the days and the kilometers passed, circumstance and serendipity recast the Camino, altering my understanding of my motives almost without my being aware of it. What had begun as an adventure, an escape from the everyday, had turned into an exploration of the spirit. There'd been no particular revelation, but I felt a kind of lift, a heightened sense that I could walk forever. More crucially, I wanted to. That seemed enough for me—and even more than I'd anticipated.

Early in the afternoon, I ambled through the hamlet of Brea with its half-dozen stone and thatch-roofed houses. Just beyond Brea was a short concrete pillar on the right side of the trail that indicated only one hundred kilometers farther to Santiago. The knowledge startled me. I hadn't forgotten about my goal, but I'd stopped thinking about getting there—or, more accurately, stopped fretting about getting there. But the fact that I'd covered nearly seven hundred kilometers surprised me. Three weeks earlier, beset by blisters and self-doubt, I'd wondered if I would have to pack it in. Now I had maybe four or five days to go. How had I done that?

I followed the path downhill through the village of Morgade and stopped to rest by a small circular fountain on the edge of town. The spigot in the center wasn't working, but the basin held a foot or so of water. I dropped my pack against the fountain wall and undid the bandana around my neck to dip it in the water and wash my face and neck. Then I found a clean patch of grass on one side of the fountain near a chestnut tree and stretched out with my back against the stone. I sipped at my water bottle and stared up at the swaying branches, listening to the chatter of linnets and swallowtails and letting the warmth of the sun bathe my body.

I might have fallen asleep but for a loud splash from the fountain. I stood up and saw ripples spreading across the surface of the water. At first I couldn't see what had made the splash. But then, as I was about to sit down again, the shiny green head of a lizard rose to the surface. It paddled to the edge and tried to climb the concrete wall. The stones were too wet and slippery, and it kept sliding back into the water.

I remembered the roadside well near Nájera and the pale bloated bellies of dead frogs floating in the dark water. I took off my boots and socks, rolled up my pants, and climbed into the fountain. The water came halfway up my calves. The lizard thrashed madly away when I tried to scoop it up with my hat. I lunged after it, only to have my feet go out from under me on the slick stone basin. I sat down with a splash. I looked for the lizard and was afraid I'd sat on it. But no, there it was on the far side of the fountain scrambling at the wall again. I got to my feet and splashed across the fountain after the creature. Clearly, the lizard didn't know I wasn't going to eat it. It kept trying to paddle away. But its movements grew more and more feeble and sluggish. I was finally able to scoop all six inches of it into the bowl of my hat.

I stepped out of the fountain, thinking I was lucky nobody from the village had been there to watch a stupid pilgrim taking a bath in his clothes. My pants and most of my shirt were soaking wet. I set my hat on the grass, tilting it so the lizard could escape. I watched it while I stripped off my shirt and draped it across a bush to dry. Instead of darting away, the creature lay on its side in my hat, its pale belly heaving, but neither its tail nor its turquoise-green head moved. I wondered if I'd exhausted it to the point of death. But then suddenly the tail twitched. The lizard jerked upright on its feet and scuttled out of my hat and across the open ground into a gap in the bramble hedge. Just before it disappeared, it stopped, head swiveled in my direction and eyes blinking.

"De nada," I said. You're welcome.

I sprawled out on the grass once again to let the sun dry my pants. I stared into the hedge after the lizard. My mind soon spun an anthropomorphic fantasy. I imagined the lizard reappearing with his doting family and hailing me as Lord Pilgrim, Protector of Lizards and Sundry Helpless Things. Or maybe he would have a lizard daughter whom I had only to kiss and she would turn into a beautiful princess; we'd spend our lives together walking the Camino hand in hand, saving lizards and frogs—and perhaps even dogs.

Lost in fantasy, I felt the green world close in around me. My ears hummed with the cacophony of birdsong. The leaves rustled with each shift in the breeze. The air, redolent with the odors of cows and sheep, enveloped me. The warmth of the sun saturated my skin. I felt myself sinking into the earth, as if I were returning home. But all of a sudden, the sensation of disappearing was gone, and like a cork bobbing to the surface, I popped free, floating out of my own body. I felt a sense of utter stillness. I was in the world but not of the world. The sensation didn't last long—a few seconds at most; but for those few moments everything was intensely real, as though some translucent membrane had been peeled away from my eyes and I was seeing the world more vividly than I had in decades. Then it was over, and I was back in my body, restored to the normal subdued presence of the world.

The experience wasn't a complete surprise. I'd had a few similar epiphanies in the past, brief moments when I was intensely aware of my surroundings even while feeling detached from them. Once, as a boy of nine or ten watching my grandfather work at his carpentry bench, I became entranced by the wood shavings that curled out of his hand plane and spiraled to the floor in a pool of sunlight. Suddenly, I felt pulled out of my body so that I was looking down on myself watching the sunlit shavings. It was, as I came to understand years later, my first experience of self-consciousness, in the philosophical sense—the intense if paradoxical awareness of myself in the world even while, at the same time, I felt somehow separate from it. Again, as a teenager, I once stood on the edge of a highway overlooking a lake when, out of the blue, I felt suddenly lifted out of myself as everything around me—the lake, trees, flowers, creaking cicadas—stood out in sharp and vivid relief.

I'd never forgotten those moments, but over time my memory of them had faded to the point where I sometimes wondered if they'd really happened or were something I'd only dreamed. Now, decades later, the Camino had reawakened me to the reality of those experiences. I don't know how long I sat against the fountain, playing the epiphany over in my mind even as the intensity of it faded. But by the time it occurred to me that I'd better get dressed because I still had a couple of hours of walking ahead of me, my shirt and pants were nearly dry. Still, I was reluctant to leave. I felt that in a sense I had just completed my pilgrimage, and I wanted to savor that feeling. What finally prompted me to leave was the growling of my stomach, reminding me that I still hadn't had anything to eat. I realized I was actually hungry.

I put my shirt back on, laced up my boots, and shouldered my pack. I took a last look around my little bower—the fountain, the trees, the gap in the hedge where the lizard had disappeared. Some long-remembered lines from one of Bashō's haiku flitted across my mind: "In this hush profound, / Into the very rocks it seeps— / The cicada sound." Along with them came another phrase attributed to Bashō, "a glimpse of the underglimmer."[3] Together, they seemed appropriate for the occasion.

The remainder of the afternoon carried me down tree-lined trails and narrow country roads through a series of hamlets that were little more than scattered farmhouses along the edge of the Camino. They smelled of hay, manure, and wood smoke. Half-lost among the chestnut, birch, and oak trees, the Camino was sometimes reduced to a cow path between thickets of wild roses, blueberry patches, and banks of ferns. The biggest hazard was the cattle droppings. Stone walls half-buried beneath moss and vines crisscrossed farm fields. Broad-horned oxen stared at me from behind paddocks. A woman dressed in black, watching a herd of sheep, crossed herself as I passed. It struck me that this part of the Camino wouldn't have looked much different five hundred years ago. I imagined the ghosts of pilgrims past crowding around me as I walked. Someday, I thought, I'd be the ghostly companion of some future pilgrim.[4]

Late in the afternoon, I crossed the long bridge over the Río Miño and climbed a steep set of stairs to the town of Portomarín, arriving in the middle of a fiesta, the Fiesta de Aguardiente. Portomarín was once a major pilgrim stop along the banks of the river. The Knights Templar maintained a garrison in the town to keep the roads free of bandits. In the 1950s, the Spanish government flooded the original town in order to build a hydroelectric dam upriver. They built a new town on the hillside above the man-made lake, recreating the ancient main street with its long arcades. The Romanesque Church of San Nicolas was also rebuilt, stone by stone.

I checked out the local refugio, but it was full. I couldn't figure out where all the pilgrims had come from since I hadn't seen any of them on the trail, and I wondered if I'd taken the wrong path. It wouldn't have been the first time. The *hospitalero* explained that the fiesta brought a lot of cycling pilgrims to town. Recommending that I try one of the hotels, he was kind enough to phone to see if any rooms were available. The gods were gracious once again. I got a room at the Posada El Camino on Calle de Lugo. The hotel was a bit run-down, but my room was warm and dry and had a small balcony overlooking the Plaza Mayor. The square, I noticed, was already crowded. People had gathered in front of a stage where members of a band were tuning their instruments. Others were eating and drinking at the long rows of cloth-covered tables in the middle of the plaza. The food stalls that encircled the square were doing a brisk business.

Despite my hunger, I took my time with the end-of-day rituals. I draped my sweaty pants and shirt on the radiator. I washed my socks and hung them to dry. And I scraped the mud and manure off my boots, wiping them as clean as I could. The treads, I noticed, were nearly smooth and the sole on the right boot was loose at the toe. After my shower I dressed in the driest clothes I had, jammed my feet back into the damp boots, and then hustled downstairs.

I strolled among the food stalls, checking the smoking braziers crammed with pots of simmering *pulpo*, or octopus. Several stalls had tall bronze *distilerías* for making the fiery brandy-like liquor known as *aguardiente*, a regional specialty. The stall owner dumped batches of fruit into a large lidded bowl on top of the apparatus while a fire burned at the bottom of it. A spigot with a tap protruded from the middle for draining the liquor. The sugary smell of burning fruit and the pungent aromas of food filled the plaza. My stomach rumbled. I was nervous about eating after my bout of food poisoning, but I needed food and drink, not necessarily in that order. I chose a stall with a long line, figuring the locals knew what was good.

"Pulpo, por favor," I said when I reached the head of the line. It was a redundant request since octopus was the only thing available—that and the *aguardiente*.

"Aquí, aquí," the man at the brazier replied, handing me a heaping pile of pepper-dressed octopus on a large wooden platter and a big chunk of bread. The woman in charge of the *distilería* filled a large mug with *aguardiente*, dropped a slice of lemon into the tawny liquid, and sprinkled sugar on top.

With food and drink in hand, I made my way into the square to find a seat at one of the tables, nodding to the others who made room for me.

"Gracias. Buenas tardes," I said.

"Hola," they greeted me in unison, nodding or raising their drinks before returning to their food.

The octopus was spicy and hot and swimming in olive oil. I finished quickly, cleaning the platter with chewy pieces of flour-dusted bread. The *aguardiente* was sweet with a burnt-sugar taste. It went down just fine, leaving a lovely lava-flow of heat in my chest. I went back for seconds. Afterwards, I sipped my drink and nibbled on a *tarta de Santiago*, the almond tart that's a specialty of the region, as I listened to the music and watched the dancing.

The music was pure Celtic—all stirring fiddles, wailing bagpipes, and haunting flutes. As darkness fell, the burning braziers cast a flickering light that turned the crowd into a mass of shifting silhouettes. I thought of marionettes in a shadow play. The wall of the church glowed with the light from the plaza, as it had no doubt done for hundreds of years. Maybe it was the drink, but as I watched the dancing crowd and listened to the music, it was easy to slip through a fissure in time to the medieval world.

I decided against a third mug of *aguardiente*, preferring to take another walk through the streets and get a long overdue café con leche at the Café Venecia. The bar was crowded, smoky, and noisy, which normally I would have enjoyed. But I was tired, and after finishing my coffee I returned to the hotel. I fell asleep to the sound of the music as shadows danced on the walls of my room.

That night I dreamt I was walking with my father on a rocky beach by an ocean. We had picked our way through a maze of boulders, stepping carefully as we headed to the shoreline. I was happy to see him, and surprised, because he was dead. I asked him what it was like to be dead and if death was something to fear. His response was lost in the roar of the waves. I then saw a child farther down the beach, playing at the water's edge. It was Chonina, the little girl in Ponferrada. She was plucking scallop shells from the sand and putting them in a red plastic bucket. I recognized the bucket. It was the same one I'd had as a child. How did she get my bucket? I walked toward her, telling my father to stay where he was and I would be back. Tendrils of fog curled around the boulders, shrouding the beach. I lost sight of Chonina, but somehow I heard her voice over the pounding waves. I ran toward her, even though I couldn't see her. I looked back at my father, but he was lost from sight. I didn't know which way to go. I didn't want to lose him again, but I had to reach Chonina. Her voice was fading, and I felt a rising panic as the waves grew louder. I didn't know what to do. That's when I woke up.

I threw back the covers and sat up in bed. I was drenched in sweat, and for a few seconds I didn't know where I was. But gradually I recognized the room and realized I'd been dreaming. Even so, I sat on the edge of the bed for a minute as images from the dream continued to flash on the screen in my head. The tide of anxiety ebbed. The coolness of the night air made me shiver, so I wrapped myself in a blanket and walked across the room to close the window. That's when I heard the flute.

I pulled the tall shutters wide open to look out over the plaza. It was still dark, but in the glow of some of the braziers I saw five people sitting at a table in front of the empty stage. One man was playing a flute. I stood on the balcony in the damp night air, listening to the haunting notes echoing through the square. I remembered my dream and thought of my father. And for the first time in decades I started to cry. It seemed a strange and wondrous thing: to be in a hotel room in a Spanish town at 5 a.m., crying over a dream that featured my long-dead father, whom I still missed, and a little girl I'd met only a few days earlier. The Camino had given me another gift: a chance to discover, or recover, the most necessary things of life, even if only in dreams.[5]

The music stopped. Someone laughed in the darkness. I wiped my eyes with a corner of the blanket. Then I was laughing, too, as the line from Lesley Gore's song from the 1960s popped into my head: "It's my party and I'll cry if I want to." I adapted the lyric: It's my Camino and I'll cry if I want to.

In that moment I had the same feeling I'd had earlier in the day after my rescue of the lizard: my pilgrimage seemed to have come to some sort of conclusion. I'd continue on to Santiago, but I felt that I had now found a sense of meaning and purpose in walking the Camino. There was no stunning revelation or conversionary epiphany—just the simple sense that in spiritual terms I'd fulfilled the purpose of my pilgrimage and crossed some sort of threshold that divided my past from what remained of my future.

I pulled a chair to the window and sat down, wrapped in the blanket, and watched the darkness retreat with the approach of daylight. The flute player resumed, and the music kept me company until the birds started to sing.

The remaining days of my Camino passed all too quickly, a kaleidoscope of image and sensation: a wayside cross and a view of green fields as I crested a hill near Sierra de Ligonde; the drum of rain as I took shelter beneath the canopy of a bus stop near Rosario; sitting on a bench and eating an orange beside a fat-trunked palm tree in the public gardens in Melide; drinking from a fountain in Boente, the water so cold my teeth ached. But I do remember one situation in particular.

After leaving Portomarín I walked to Palas do Rei and stayed overnight. The next day I hiked the thirty kilometers to Arzúa. There I got a second-floor room at the Casa Frade on Calle Ramón Franco. An elderly couple, Nemesio Hortal and Hescates Sanmartin, ran the place. The room they gave me made me think I'd stepped back half a century or more. It was lovely. The large bed was piled with quilts. The chairs, dresser, and stand-alone wardrobe were made of dark mahogany. The dresser mirror was pure art deco, the kind of beveled glass you see only in expensive antique shops in North America. A glass-enclosed balcony, with two wicker chairs and a small table, overlooked the street. I was the only guest that day, and I had the dining room—with its heavy wood chairs and lace-fringed tablecloths—to myself at suppertime. On the walls, watching me, were photographs of men, women, and children dressed in black clothes that, so far as I could tell, dated to the late 1800s. They reminded me of family pictures on the walls of my grandparents' home in Hanna, Alberta, that used to scare me as a boy.

My hosts served me *caldo gallego*, the Galician vegetable soup, as well as beef stew and a basket of freshly baked bread, along with a bottle of cold Albariño white wine. The soup was flavored with dill, which triggered even more memories of sitting in my grandmother's kitchen as a boy, gulping her soup of potatoes and sour cream with sprigs of fresh dill and anticipating her apple coffee cake dripping with syrup and cinnamon and the juice of the apples.

There was no coffee cake after the meal, but Nemesio brought a small burner and a shallow pan to the table and explained that he was going to prepare *queimada*, known as the "fire drink" of Galicia. He lit the burner and tipped a bottle of *orujo* liquor into the pan, filling it to just below the rim. While the liquor was heating, Hescates carefully stirred in shredded lemon peel, sugar, and some crushed coffee beans. Nemesio let the liquor heat for several minutes and then turned off the burner. He took a ladle-like spoon and scooped the warm liquor into a small clay jug, which he then poured into three ceramic cups. Nemesio and Hescates took their cups and gestured for me to take mine.

"Su salud," said Nemesio, knocking the drink back.

"Salud," I said, imitating him.

The drink had a good kick to it and burned down my throat with a sharp bite of the coffee. It went well with the fat cigar Nemesio offered me—in Spain, you don't refuse the offer of a cigarette or a cigar even if you don't smoke. While Hescates cleared away the plates, Nemesio and I smoked cigars together until he excused himself and joined his wife in the kitchen. I took my cigar, along with the bottle of white wine, up to my room. I sat in one of the wicker chairs in the enclosed balcony, listening to the pattern of rain on the glass and watching people come and go from the bar across the street. I had no urge to join them. I was happy to be alone with my thoughts and memories. As darkness fell, I finished the wine and the cigar and then went to bed.

In the morning, Hescates gave me a large bowl of café con leche and a fresh baguette smeared with butter and jam. Nemesio brought me the bill: 3,000 pesetas, or about $30. I'd have paid more just for having the memory of my grandmother revived.

After Arzúa, I put in a strenuous day climbing up and down steep hills across a series of river valleys on the way to Lavacolla. Outside Salceda, I passed the memorial to Guillermo Watt, the sixty-nine-year-old pilgrim who died of a heart attack in 1993, one day away from Santiago. In memory of the man, a pair of bronzed shoes had been set in a niche in the stone wall at the side of the Camino.

For the most part, I walked with my own memories. Certainly I was immersed in and aware of the sensory world around me as I traipsed through forests of poplar and pine and eucalyptus, climbed up and down hills, splashed through puddles and streams, and followed sandy pathways, narrow lanes, and minor roads through farm hamlets—Ras, Santa Irena, Arca—until, finally, I reached Lavacolla. But I also wandered in the realm of the past. I was in two places at once.[6] It was as if my psyche understood that my Camino would soon come to an end and this might be the last opportunity I'd have to spend so much uninterrupted time walking through my own memories.

I enjoyed a geographical pastiche of my life: a kibbutz in northern Israel near the Golan just after the Yom Kippur War; a tent commune along the Moroccan coast near Agadir; a tiny attic room in a Paris apartment building near Place d'Italie; a house on Ravensbourne Road in the London suburb of Bromley; a room with a big bay window on Burdett Avenue in Victoria.

One memory, in particular, surprised me because I didn't realize I'd forgotten it. Walking along a eucalyptus-lined road between Arzúa and Lavacolla, I suddenly remembered going with my father and his friend—I called him Uncle Bill—on a fishing trip in the Rocky Mountains west of Red Deer. I was maybe seven or eight years old. It was dark, and we were sitting by the campfire. In the flash of memory, I was staring into the fire, happy to be staying up so late and sitting beside my dad. Eventually, though, he told me it was time to go to bed, and I reluctantly went into the tent and crawled into my sleeping bag. I fought off sleep, wanting desperately to be back outside with them around the campfire and wishing my father understood that. I got out of the sleeping bag and peered through the mesh window on the side of the tent.

My father and Uncle Bill were sitting on logs opposite each other, silhouetted against the light of the fire. Bill had a beer to his lips, while my father was sitting hunched forward, elbows on his knees, staring into the fire, with a beer bottle in his hands. He was saying something.

This tableau of the two men was so vivid in my mind that I came to a halt on the trail, afraid to walk further lest my movement shatter the image. For a moment I heard the crackling of the campfire and smelled the canvas of the tent wall and tried to make out what my father was saying. Standing on the Camino beneath a eucalyptus tree, I strained across the chasm of decades to hear my father's long-lost words. My throat tightened and my eyes filled. I took a deep breath to break the spell, letting go of whatever it was I'd been trying to hear. I hadn't thought of that fishing trip for decades—hadn't even realized it was stored among my memories. As I jabbed my walking stick into the ground and resumed walking, I wondered why, of all the possible memories, that was the one that had come to mind.

It was late afternoon by the time I reached Lavacolla, where, as tradition has it, pilgrims once washed in the river and made themselves presentable before walking into Santiago. I'd walked some thirty kilometers. My legs ached, and my back was sore. I thought of stopping for the day. It had been threatening rain, and storm clouds were gathering. But it was only another ten kilometers to Santiago—a couple of hours at the most. I suddenly wanted to finish the Camino. With luck the rain might hold off for a couple of hours.

No such luck. Just outside San Marcos, a deluge hit. One moment I was contemplating the greenery, lost in memory, and the next I was completely wet, not having bothered to put on my rain jacket. The rain came down so hard it ricocheted off the roadway to form a curtain of ground-level spray. My boots and pants were soaked. A sheet of lightning lit up the sky, followed almost immediately by a great crack of thunder. It was so loud my ears hurt. I ducked instinctively. Time to run, I figured. It would be embarrassing to be killed by lightning a couple of hours shy of finishing my pilgrimage. Surely the gods weren't that black-humored.

Up ahead, through the wall of rain, I saw a small chapel. It stood at the bottom of a knoll on top of which was a large crucifix. It was Monte del Gozo, the Mount of Joy, where, in centuries past, pilgrims had their first sight of the towers of Santiago.[7] Just then, I didn't care about sightseeing. I just wanted to get out of the rain.

Under the eaves of the chapel, I waited for half an hour for the rain to let up sufficiently before I could climb the hill to stand at the foot of the cross. In the heavy mist and rain I couldn't make out the towers of the cathedral in Santiago. Instead, just below me, I saw rows and rows of barracks-like buildings. This was the huge refugio built by the Xunta de Galicia in 1993, which the Catholic Church declared as a Holy Year for celebrating the faith. It can accommodate more than three thousand people, offering—in addition to the refugio—a campsite, restaurants, bars, and huge parking lots. Welcome back to civilization, I thought. Regardless of the rain, there was no way I was going to stay at such a place.

And so it was that in the early evening, thirty-two days after leaving Saint-Jean-Pied-de-Port, I crossed the bridge over the Autopista del Atlantico, stumbled through the suburb of San Lázaro and across the busy intersection at Avenida de Lugo, climbed uphill along the Calle Fuente de los Concheiros, passing the small square with the cross of Homo Sancto, and walked along Rúa de San Pedro to the Porto do Camiño, as it's known in Galicia—the traditional pilgrim entry point into the old city of Santiago de Compostela.[8]

Even when I thought my pilgrimage was complete, the Camino still had a small surprise in store for me. Standing at the intersection of Rúa de San Pedro and Rúa das Rodas, waiting for the light to change, feeling slightly shell-shocked at the traffic, and glancing up and down the street, what did I spot near the curb at my feet but some orange peels scattered among other debris. No way, I thought. I suppose I could have gone rooting in the gutter to see if they bore the neatly sliced style of the Orange-Peel Man, but the light changed. I crossed the street and entered the old city, leaving the peels for the street sweepers. I decided to take it on faith that the Camino was granting me a final salutary gesture.

But I was wrong. My pilgrimage wasn't quite over.

9

DISAPPEARANCE

We must be still and still moving
Into another intensity.
T. S. ELIOT, "EAST COKER,"
IN *FOUR QUARTETS*

The tolling of bells awakened me. Voices and laughter drifted up from the street and through the window of my room. Somewhere in the distance I heard the plaintive wail of bagpipes. It was dark. I lay on the bed, trying to fathom the fact that I'd actually walked—okay, mostly walked—the Camino de Santiago.

I had reached the city a couple of hours earlier, after walking for about forty kilometers—the longest stretch of my pilgrimage. I wobbled with fatigue. Wandering the labyrinth of cobblestone streets, I eventually stumbled into Rúa do Vilar where by coincidence, or so it seemed, the woman who owned the *hospedaje* where I was now napping found me leaning uncertainly and half-asleep against the tall green doors of her *pensión*.

"Perdón, señor," she said, snapping me out of my weariness. I heard her ask if I was looking for a room.

"Sí, señora. ¿Una habitación con una ducha caliente?"

"Aquí, aquí."

The doors I'd been leaning against turned out to be the entrance for the Hospedaje Santa Cruz. María, who runs the *pensión*, also owned a small grocery shop farther up the street. For years, as I later learned, she has kept an eye out for weary pilgrims. I followed her up two flights of stairs to the room, wondering if it was coincidence or serendipity that had brought me to her door. Or perhaps it was God taking care of fools and pilgrims. The room was clean and dry. It had a big bed, a large wardrobe, and a small battered desk against one wall. A tall window with shutters overlooked the street. There was a shower down the hall. I took the room for about twenty dollars a night.

When María left I dropped my pack on the floor and sat on the bed, just to get the weight off my feet. I made the mistake of leaning back against the pillows and stretching my legs out on the bed. The next thing I knew I was awake and hearing the sound of bells and bagpipes. I glanced at my watch. It was nearly 9 p.m. I thought about taking off my still-damp clothes and wet boots and crawling under the covers, but my stomach was growling. Besides, my arrival in Santiago demanded some sort of celebration. I wanted a nice meal, a bottle of cold white wine, and—to toast the completion of my pilgrimage—a large single malt Scotch.

I didn't completely abandon my pilgrim discipline. I hung up my wet clothes, cleaned my boots, and poured the remains of my water bottle on my much-loved Hillmaster and wiped it clean, offering it a thank-you blessing for having fended off aggressive dogs, dispersed chickens from my path, and kept me upright on more than a few slippery slopes. Then I had my shower and put on dry clothes, grabbed my rain jacket and the satchel containing my notebooks and journal and guidebook, and headed for the door. I left the walking stick in the corner with my pack.

Without knowing where I'd end up, I walked along Rúa do Vilar to the Praza das Platerías, the Square of Silversmiths, with its fountain of four horse heads, and across the Praza da Quintana. Climbing a set of wide stone steps that bisected the square took me past the Café Literarios, its tables crowded with students from the university, and into the Praza da Inmaculada. Then, passing through an arched tunnel and into the enormous Praza do Obradoiro, I found the cathedral, its western facade and twin baroque towers illuminated by spotlights. It was truly stunning.

I remembered reading that Gabriel García Márquez, the Colombian novelist, had once described the Praza do Obradoiro as "the most beautiful square" in the world.[1] I wasn't going to quarrel with that judgment. I stared at the massive, elaborately sculptured facade of the cathedral with its twin towers climbing into the sky and the wide double staircase that leads to the Pórtico da Gloria—the Doorway of Glory—and to the church's interior. I planned to attend the Pilgrims' Mass at noon the next day, after a haircut and a shave and some new clothes.

The bells in the cathedral's towers tolled 10 p.m., filling the square with a stentorian bong that vibrated through my chest. Even this late, the square was full of people—buskers playing bagpipes, pilgrims in their shabby pants and boots, and tourists in loud clothes and sandals—but it was too large to feel crowded. I stopped to listen to the bagpipers and to watch a mime entertain a group of spectators.

I exited the plaza at the top of Rúa do Franco, a narrow street lined with bars and restaurants. I followed the jostling crowd, pausing to read the menus in the windows or to look at aquariums teeming with lobsters, crabs, squids, eels, and oysters. Finally, after walking up and down the street twice, I decided on El Cayado, mainly because the woman behind the bar smiled at me when I stuck my head in the doorway.

"¿Peregrino?" she asked.

"Sí."

"¡Entre! ¡Entre!" She waved me inside, directed me to a small table, and gestured to a waiter to set it. The waiter was a short bald man dressed in a white shirt, black vest, and black bow tie. He seemed pleased when I conveyed that I would rely on his recommendations for what to eat and drink. The only thing I insisted on ordering was a large single malt Scotch for after the meal. "Whisky de malta. Después de la comida. ¿Entiende?" He seemed to understand my inadequate Spanish.

Soon my waiter returned with a big white tureen and ladled out *sopa de mariscos*, making sure my bowl was swimming with clams, shrimp, and oysters. He uncorked a chilled bottle of Alcorta wine, letting me test it—sharp, tart, and very dry—before filling my glass. I was very hungry. I finished the tureen and had two servings of *pulpo con cachelas*, paprika-seasoned octopus, soaking up the juice with the last chunks of bread.

My hunger sated, and with a tumbler of Glenfiddich to nurse, I watched idly as the waiters put fresh sheets of white paper on the vacated tables, folding the corners with a sharp crease. Many of the diners were parents with their children, or young couples who had eyes only for each other. It was noisy with the clatter of cutlery and conversation, yet I felt as if I were seeing and hearing all of it from a distant shore.

I should have felt at peace with my mission accomplished, my pilgrimage signed, sealed, and delivered. I had that feeling, to be sure, but it bumped up against a bout of the blues. It didn't take much for me to figure out why. For the first time in a month I didn't know what I was going to do the next day. For the last four weeks I'd had the Camino waiting for me in the morning. But now what? It was hard to believe I no longer needed to rise in the morning and walk twenty or thirty kilometers, rain or shine. I wouldn't have to inspect my feet for blisters or swollen tendons. I wouldn't have to wash my socks in tiny sinks or clean mud and manure off my boots. I wouldn't have to listen to the snores of pilgrims in damp and moldy refugios. Yet, oddly, I didn't feel so much relieved as homesick. I'd grown used to walking for hours on end each day. No longer having to meet that requirement was a shock to my system. I was already lonely for the Camino. A month of walking had turned me into a pilgrim. Was I now simply a tourist?

I was well aware that my post-pilgrimage blues were common. The shift from pilgrim to non-pilgrim status has psychological consequences, including, as I'd read, *la gran depresión del Camino*. The great depression of the Camino is a paradoxical mix of letdown, fatigue, relief, and restlessness.[2]

Images from the Camino crowded my mind: the pleasant walk out of Roncesvalles to Espinal on my second day; sunlight on the wet steps of a church in Navarrete; those moments of deep silence on the *meseta* outside Hontanas; the children playing in the square in Santo Domingo de la Calzada; the lizard lying motionless in my hat; and the flute player in Portomarín. Sipping my Scotch, I envisioned a parade of faces of the people I'd met during the past month: Gerard, Anne, Henrik, Ron, Andrea, and Jesús. I thought of Chonina and imagined my scallop shell among the treasures of her childhood.

I knew then that I'd spend months trying to piece the mosaic of my pilgrimage into some coherent pattern, trying to understand what the Camino meant to me. I already understood that my pilgrimage had been an escape of sorts. It had uprooted me from my daily life, from all the routines and obligations and habits that make up my normal existence. But it had been more than that, too. I'd journeyed along the Camino, but the Camino had also journeyed through me.[3] It had chipped away the carapace of my everyday reality, uncovering memories, dreams, and reflections that had lain hidden beneath the sediments of career and consumption. Part of me didn't want to return to my so-called real life, with all its deadening diversions. I wanted to keep walking in order to excavate more of my buried life. I wanted to burn away the dross of decades, strip down until I found the hard kernel of my self.

A mad thought dashed across my mind: I would become a permanent pilgrim. I'd heard of men who did just that, men who, after walking the Camino once, couldn't return to their previous lives and walked back and forth along the road, sometimes for years. I pictured myself trekking between Roncesvalles and Santiago, season after season, my hair growing long and white, my body lean and tough, until, in a kind of resurrection, I burned off all the sloth and sloppiness of my former self. The dogs would learn to recognize me and no longer bark. I'd dedicate myself to saving frogs and lizards. I'd lose my job, certainly, but who knows what I might gain? Who knows what another month, another year, another decade of pilgrimage might bring forth? Madness or revelation? Or perhaps a greater sanity?

A burst of laughter from a child at a nearby table snapped me out of my fantasy. No, it was not my fate to be a peripatetic saint, crazy or otherwise. I had promises to keep, duties to perform, and bills to pay. Yet I had to admit to the temptation of the idea that if I just kept walking, the world would take care of me.

With my meal finished and the whiskey polished off, I was suddenly tired. I looked around the restaurant. The families with children were gone, replaced by groups of students. They were too loud and too young for me. I'd hear them in the early morning as they staggered up the narrow streets, singing and laughing. I walked back to my room and slipped into bed just as the cathedral's bells rang midnight. As I drifted into sleep, I realized I'd become fond of hearing church bells. I was going to miss them, too.

I didn't miss them the next morning, though. They sounded as if they were right outside my window. It was 7 a.m. I could have stayed in bed longer, but my body told me it was time to move. I obeyed, wondering how long the discipline would hold.

I spent the morning restoring myself to post-Camino life. I got a haircut and a shave at the Tourino Peluqueros salon on Rúa da Senra. The barber was a woman, and to have her shampoo and cut my hair, brush on the lather and scrape away the stubble, and drape a hot towel over my face was as close to sexual pleasure as I'd known in more than a month. I left her a large tip.

I found a men's store on Rúa da Caldeirería and bought a shirt, a pair of slacks, and sandals. I was surprised at how much weight I'd lost—at least thirty pounds, judging by the sales clerk's measurements. Seeing myself in the mirror in the changing room, I certainly looked a lot healthier. My eyes were bright and my face browned and hollowed by a month outdoors.

I'd had nothing to read for a month besides my two volumes of poetry and my journal and guidebooks. I was desperate for something different, preferably a novel. In a bookstore near Praza do Toural I found a couple of shelves of English-language books. The selection was limited. I was about to settle for a Muriel Spark novel when I spotted a copy of Michael Dibdin's *Dead Lagoon*. Perfect. After Mass I would find a bar and enjoy the adventures of the world-weary Italian police detective, Aurelio Zen, on the hunt for a murderer in Venice.

I went to the pilgrims' office on Rúa do Vilar to show my *credencial* and to collect the cathedral's certificate of pilgrimage, the *compostelana*, that attested to my having completed the Camino. Technically, you only have to walk the last hundred kilometers of the Camino to qualify for pilgrim status. Filling out the forms, the young priest asked about my motive for the pilgrimage. "Espiritualidad," I said without hesitation. Spirituality.

While the priest completed my *compostelana* I read the testimonials of other pilgrims in the cathedral register. "Thank you, Spain, for a wonderful experience," wrote two pilgrims, Margaret and Michael Isaac, from New Zealand. "We are very sad our Camino is finished." "What a wonderful sense of quiet calm attends you walking the Way of St. James," wrote an Australian woman, Sue Gardner. "It is indeed a special experience that will remain important for the rest of my life." One entry in particular caught my eye. "Twenty-two days walked from Roncesvalles to Santiago, an experience of experiencing the Lord in nature, in the pilgrim path, in the people, in the churches, in everything. I experience God everywhere." The signature was that of Father Hector Pinto from Gujarat, India.

And now, I thought, I've joined all those who had come before me, one among millions over the centuries who walked across Spain to Santiago. I wrote my name in the book. Only I couldn't think of anything to equal Pinto's words. I had no such faith, try as I might. But then I thought of some lines from R. S. Thomas, one of the poets who'd kept me company on the Camino. "Prompt me, God . . . Though it be you who speak through me / Something is lost / The meaning is in the waiting."[4] It seemed to me that if any words expressed what I'd learned about my motives for walking the Camino, capturing both my longing and my lacking as a pilgrim, it was that last line. So that's what I wrote in the register.

The priest handed me the *compostelana*. It was written in Latin on heavy pinkish paper the size of an ordinary letter, embossed with the image of St. James and the seal of the Cathedral of Santiago, and decorated with elaborate scrollwork around the edges. I had no idea what it said.

"Gracias, padre."

"De nada," the priest replied. "You have walked the Way of Santiago. You are a *peregrino*. May God be with you."

I left the office and walked up the street to the Hotel Suso to have a café con leche. Then returning to my hotel to shed my pilgrimage clothes, I put on my new shirt, slacks, and sandals and walked to the Praza do Obradoiro. It seemed even larger during the day and certainly more crowded. Priests in long robes strolled across the square, hands clasped behind their backs. Mothers pushed carriages. Children ran laughing between the groups of old men who stood talking and gesticulating. Tourists huddled around buses parked at the edge of the square. I spotted several pilgrims with their backpacks, walking staffs, and dirty clothes. I didn't recognize any of them. Above us all loomed the spires of the cathedral.

Santiago has a well-earned reputation for being one of the rainiest cities in Spain. According to my research, the locals see about thirty days of sunshine a year. Not surprisingly, they have made their circumstances a point of pride, arguing that the city's beauty comes forth in the rain. That's accurate. I certainly liked the way moss grew thick and green on the walls of buildings, the way patinas of lichens clung to the chain-linked bollards, and the way micro-gardens sprouted in cracks in the stone. In the summer, I'd read, gardeners climb the walls of the cathedral to hoe vegetation from the towers and belfries, showering the plaza below with pink valerian and yellow ragwort.[5] But my favorite moments in Santiago, when it seemed to me the city really displayed its glories, were when the rain ceased and the sun broke through, causing the streets and buildings to glow.

Squatting on one of the bollards near the posh Hostal de los Reyes Católicos on one side of the plaza, I thought about some of the history I'd read. In the Middle Ages hundreds of people from across Europe camped in the city's square, pitching tents around huge bonfires. Communal meals were cooked in enormous pots. Women had babies by the light of the flames. Prostitutes plied their trade. By some accounts, riots, fights, stabbings, and even murders in and around the cathedral were common.[6] Yet the great plaza also attracted many of the kings and queens of Christendom, along with the likes of St. Francis of Assisi, Lorenzo de Medici, El Cid, Margery Kempe, St. Brigitta of Sweden, Jan van Eyck, and Geoffrey Chaucer's Wife of Bath, if you can include a fictional character.

When it started to drizzle I crossed the plaza, climbed the wide staircase to the main doors of the cathedral, and entered the Pórtico da Gloria that led to the nave. The alcove wasn't too crowded, so I pulled my research journal out of my satchel and read my notes about the Doorway of Glory as I studied it. It was carved from brown granite between 1168 and 1188 and has five columns that support three symmetrical arches. Each arch is elaborately decorated with hundreds of carvings that depict a who's who of the Bible, from Adam and Eve and the Old Testament figures to Jesus Christ, St. James, and the twenty-four elderly musicians who, according to Revelation, are booked to play at the Triumph of the Apocalypse.[7] I liked what Walter Starkie wrote about the display: "All the human race past, present and future, appear in this Gate of Glory, which is both a divine drama and a symphony sculpted in stone."[8] To me, though, the Doorway of Glory also showed a deep understanding of human psychology, revealing both our animal nature and our transcendent longing. But not every figure reflected a tragic sense of life; not every face was full of solemnity and tears. Some of the figures pulsed with vitality—the throb and thrill of simply being alive. There was laughter in some of the stone faces.

My favorite figure was the smooth-faced statue of Daniel, the Old

Testament interpreter of dreams. He stood with the other bearded prophets—Moses, Isaiah, and Jeremiah—on the crown of one of the pillars. But while the other prophets had solemn faces, Daniel bore a big grin, as though he'd discovered that the cosmos, from beginning to end, was supremely funny. The End of Days, it seemed, may well be a time of joy and mirth.

Even Christ, portrayed in the central tympanum sitting on his throne and displaying his wounds, seemed to stare wide-eyed and wondrous at the world. At his feet was a life-size statue of St. James, his left hand resting on a pilgrim staff. He, too, wore a slight smile—maybe, I thought, because he didn't have to walk anymore. That was the first time I'd seen a statue of "Sant Iago" not depicting him walking or sitting on a horse and swinging a sword.

The central column beneath the arch attracted the most attention. This was the Tree of Jesse or, more formally, the Christological Column. My guidebook said it is made of white porphyry and represents the union of the human and divine origins of Christ. As I drew closer, I could see the indentation of a hand, as though someone with great strength had pushed a splayed palm into solid stone. The actual circumstances are more impressive. Hundreds of years ago, some anonymous pilgrim praying beneath the figure of St. James placed his hand against the column. Others imitated him and now, after millions of beseeching hands, there are deep indentations into which a thumb and four fingers easily fit. When my turn came, I stashed my journal back in my satchel, knelt on the floor before the pillar, and pressed my hand to the stone.

Then, like everyone else, I walked through the vast cathedral to join the line in the narrow passage behind the High Altar to await my turn to hug the gaudy, bejeweled, and lacquered statue of St. James. I tried to remember all the people on whose behalf I'd promised *un abrazo por el apóstol*: the elderly man in Santo Domingo de la Calzada who'd made the sign of the cross as I left on my journey; José, the farmer near Azofra who'd given me a lift in his rickety truck; Esperanza Nuñez Pérez, who'd provided such a lovely room in O Cebreiro; and Chonina's mother. I knew I was probably forgetting someone, so I tried a last all-inclusive hug, figuring that a saint would remember anyone I'd forgotten.

By then it was time for the *Misa de Peregrinos*, the noon-hour Pilgrims' Mass. The pews were filling up fast. By now there must have been several hundred people in the cathedral. But I found a place in the nave near the Doorway of Glory. During special Masses or on High Feast days, as I'd read, the cathedral authorities bring out the *botafu-meiro*, an eighty-kilogram, silver-plated iron censer as big as an automobile engine. Eight red-robed men controlling a system of ropes and pulleys hoist it above the worshipers. As it gains momentum, it swings back and forth, spewing clouds of smoke and incense. In the Middle Ages, the ritual was necessary to mask the smell of a cathedral jammed with pilgrims for whom bathing was a sometime thing and deodorant still a few centuries away. I would like to have seen that ceremony, but there was no *botafumeiro* on my day in the cathedral. I had to imagine what it must have been like as I listened to the priests chant the liturgy and watched the candlelight dancing on the gilded surfaces of the High Altar.

I remembered that first Mass a month ago in Roncesvalles and how awkward I'd felt. Now the kneeling and the gestures came less self-consciously as I spoke the words, "Lord, hear my prayer." I couldn't in all honesty claim to have recovered my faith. Still, I adopted a kind of Pascalian willingness to acknowledge that a transcendent order beyond the limited nature of rational human comprehension—God—was possible. And if God was possible, then it did no harm—and perhaps even some good—to act as though God existed. And so again I prayed for everyone I could think of: my son and my wife, my mother, the soul of my father, my brother and sisters, friends and lovers, past and present. I prayed for people I'd met on the Camino, or at least those I could recall just then.

I was about to stand and leave when I remembered Roberto Lado, a professor from Madrid whom I'd met in the Gare Montparnasse in Paris. We'd shared a meal and several bottles of wine on the Paris-to-Madrid train. He had insisted he was an atheist, that the gaudy gimmicks and silly superstitions of the church were fit only for peasants, not for hard-nosed existentialists. "I believe in Sartre," he'd said, laughing and banging his fist on the table so hard that the glasses rattled. But by the time we'd emptied the third bottle he was saying "I have to make my peace with God." When I staggered off the train at Bayonne, he leaned out the window and shouted, "Roberto, por favor, say a prayer for me to the apostle." So I did.

After the Mass I wandered the streets, admiring the shop-window displays of fine linens, jewelry, and pottery. In a shop on Rúa da Caldeirería I bought a silk scarf for my wife. On Praza de Cervantes I found a replica pair of dueling pistols for my son. Then I adjourned to Bar Fuco Luis on Rúa de Xelmírez, where they played light jazz and I could sit in a corner at one of the white marble-topped tables, enjoy my Estrella Galicia, and read how Aurelio Zen coped with the corruption and cynicism of Italian politics.

The lovely dark-haired woman working at the bar got me thinking about the Camino's effect on a pilgrim's sex drive. The hard slog of each day, the preoccupation with getting from one place to the next, the goal of finding food and shelter, the need to attend to blisters and sore tendons and to get enough sleep had apparently kept my mind off sex, at least for a while. Had I stumbled on the secret of monastic life? Was disciplining the body good for you, spiritually speaking, because it redirected physical desire and fostered a more transcendent longing? It seemed a reasonable notion. But what had been my concentrated focus on the pilgrimage was now succumbing to the titillations and temptations of society after less than two days back in the mundane world. Now that my basic needs were met and I had nothing serious to do, my sex drive was stirring.[9]

Tomorrow, I decided, I would take the bus to Finisterre and walk to "the end of the world"—as medieval Christendom thought of the place. The Camino, it seemed, was not only a drug but also a diversion.

It was still dark when a taxi dropped me at the bus station the next morning. I sat in the cafeteria eating freshly baked chocolate croissants and drinking small cups of thick coffee spiked with the local *aguardiente*, happy at the thought of being back on the road, even if only as a passenger and only for a day.

Finisterre is a small fishing village on the coast of northwestern Spain, about one hundred kilometers west of Santiago. Until Christopher Columbus reached the Americas in 1492, it was widely believed that beyond Finisterre lay only a trackless ocean of monsters. Officially,

Finisterre is not part of the Camino; nonetheless, many pilgrims visit the town, either on foot or by bus, after reaching Santiago. For many it is a symbolically fitting place to conclude a pilgrimage.[10]

I checked the breast pocket of my rain jacket to make sure I still had the smooth white stone that had caught my eye on a Nova Scotia beach two months earlier. Knowing then that I would soon walk the Camino, I'd picked up the stone to throw into the water on the other side of the Atlantic if I completed the pilgrimage. It struck me that my Camino had been nothing like the escapist adventure I'd imagined that day on the beach.

I finished my coffee, paid the bill, grabbed my stick, and walked down the stairs to the bus platform. I wasn't surprised to see other pilgrims waiting in line, but I was pleasantly surprised to see one I knew—Eva Lerin, the Spanish woman with whom I'd had dinner in Molinaseca.

"Hola, Eva. ¿Cómo estás?"

She recognized me. "Roberto. Bien, gracias. ¿Y usted?"

I said I was fine and asked whether she'd had a good Camino. "¿Tuviste un buen Camino?"

"Sí, era bueno."

Standing in line for the bus, we caught up on Camino news. She'd walked alone for the last several days, arriving in Santiago the previous day. She had to be back in time to catch the evening train to Madrid but didn't want to miss seeing Finisterre. We got to talking with two other pilgrims behind us in line, an elderly German couple, Helmut and Ingrid. They'd walked the Camino nearly thirty years earlier as newlyweds. Back then, they said, it was much different. There were few refugios and even fewer facilities that catered to pilgrims. They often slept in fields or, if they were lucky, on the floor of a church. Why had they returned?

"We never forgot it," said Helmut, gazing at Ingrid. "We wanted to see it again before . . ."—he paused and took his wife's hand—"before it was too late."

How soon would it be too late, and for what reason, I wondered as we boarded the bus. They sat a couple of seats in front of Eva and me. During the trip I'd occasionally look up from my novel to see Ingrid asleep with her head against Helmut's shoulder.

The bus rolled across the green hills of Galicia, through forests of eucalyptus, pine, and chestnut and past white-walled villages with their red-tile roofs. Finally, as the land opened up and I saw the ocean, there was Finisterre and its granite houses huddled at the foot of the peninsula.

I'd imagined some gloomy fog-enshrouded escarpment of crumbling stone on the edge of nowhere. Instead, the bus pulled into a pretty fishing port of narrow cobbled streets and whitewashed buildings with wrought-iron balconies bedecked with potted flowers. Dozens of brightly colored fishing boats lay at anchor in the harbor. The pungent smell of seaweed, salt water, and rotting fish greeted us as we stepped off the bus. Sea gulls cried overhead.

Cape Finisterre is about two kilometers beyond the town along a thumb of land jutting into the Atlantic Ocean. Helmut and Ingrid wanted to eat before they walked out to the cape. Eva and I decided to walk first, figuring we could get to the cape and back in time for a leisurely lunch before catching the 3 p.m. bus back to Santiago.

I was glad to be walking again, enjoying the stretch and pull of the muscles in my legs, the crunch of gravel beneath my boots, and the rhythmic tapping of my Hillmaster. I felt at home again. Eva and I followed Rúa do Alcalde Fernández out of town as it climbed a narrow tarmac road toward the cape. The ocean was spread before us—gray, heaving, white-capped, and empty except for the occasional fishing boat bobbing in the water, its bow sending up spumes of spray as it plunged into the troughs between the waves.

I'd read some of the history of the area and remembered it as I walked. Locals referred to the northwest coast of Spain as the Costa da Morte, the Coast of the Dead. In past centuries, the region's often stormy seas were notorious for shipwrecks. The townspeople congregated at the cape after a bad storm to watch for bodies and debris floating to shore. According to one legend, the waters off the coast hide the ancient city of Duyo, inundated by tidal waves on the same day in 79 AD that Mount Vesuvius erupted and buried Pompeii in ash and lava. The legend has it that on nights when the fog is especially thick and the winds howl off the ocean, you can hear the dead of Duyo crying.

In pre-Christian times, Cape Finisterre was also the site where Galicia's pagans performed Celtic sun-worshiping rites. With the advent of Christianity, pilgrims transformed the pagan rites to suit their purposes.

During medieval times, seaside rituals of prayer sometimes turned into bacchanalian orgies. Modern pilgrims, seemingly more restrained in public than their medieval counterparts, sometimes burn their Camino clothes and throw their walking sticks into the ocean. Some even go for a swim in an act of symbolic purification.[11] I thought I'd settle for tossing my white stone into the water.

There wasn't much to see at the end of the world—a cross, a lighthouse, and a café with big picture windows. We walked around large rocks at the base of the lighthouse, patted the bronze boots cemented onto a boulder, and then headed back to the café when it started to rain. A celebratory glass of wine seemed in order.

"Salud. Here's to the end of the Camino," I said, as we raised our glasses. I asked Eva why she'd enjoyed the Camino. She said she found it peaceful, just what she needed. When I asked what she meant, she told me about her recent divorce that had left her depressed, and how her father and son had urged her to make the pilgrimage.

"It is something a lot of Spanish people do," she explained. "It's better than going to a psychologist."

When I asked her how it helped, she replied, "It was being alone for so much time. You walk every day, and after a while all the things you thought were important aren't so important anymore." Eva paused and sipped her wine. "No, that's not quite right. You realize what's important."

I showed Eva the white stone and explained my end-of-the-Camino ritual. "What a good idea," she said. "I didn't bring anything with me. Next time." She said she'd walk with me along the road but didn't want to climb down to the water.

When the rain let up we walked part of the way back toward Finisterre until I found a path that zigzagged off the road and down to the shore. While Eva settled herself beside a boulder out of the wind, I stumbled down the slope to a small cove-like spot at the water's edge. I was alone except for the sea crashing on the rocks.

I wasn't going for a swim, but a bit of wading seemed appropriate as a modified purification ritual. I took off my boots and socks and rolled up my pants. The stones were cold beneath my feet. As I waded into the ocean, gasping at the frigid water, the surge of a wave against my legs soaked my pants. So much for staying dry. I took the stone out of the pocket of my jacket and rolled it around in my hands. Maybe, I fancifully imagined, the forces of geology, of shifting tectonic plates and floating continents, would someday deposit it on the shores of North America. But of course by then, I and everything I loved would be long dead.

Why was I thinking of death? I had no particular reason for feeling morbid. I tried to think of something special to say, a prayer to utter, even if I would only be talking to the indifferent ocean. Nothing came to mind. Instead, I conjured the fragments of a poem by R. S. Thomas that I'd read repeatedly for the past month. I closed my eyes and let what words I could remember come to me, reciting them to the endless waves: "There are nights so still / I lie awake listening / to the swell of the Atlantic / rising and falling, wave on wave on the shore." I stopped for a second, uncertain of the words. But then they, too, came to me: "And the thought comes of that other being awake / letting our prayers break on Him / not only for hours / but for days, years, and eternity."[12]

When I finished I looked at the white stone and then threw it as far as I could. I didn't see it fall. I stood for a few moments, waiting for . . . what? I didn't know. I turned back to the shore, retrieved my boots, and sat between boulders to get out of the wind and put them on. I took an orange from my satchel and my knife from a pocket and sliced the fruit so the peel came off in neat quarter sections. I tossed the peels into the water and watched as the tide took them away. I ate the orange and then closed my eyes to listen to the waves surge up the shore, break and recede, and then return in a grating roar.

I must have lost myself momentarily in the ceaseless ebb and flow when I heard someone call my name. I lurched to my feet. For a split second I couldn't distinguish between the roaring waves and my pounding heart, as though I didn't know where my body ended and the world began. Slowly, or so it seemed, I came back to myself and recognized Eva's voice.

"Roberto, where are you? Are you all right?"

I looked over the boulder to see her standing higher up on the slope. She'd clambered down the path I'd taken.

"When you didn't come back I thought something had happened," she said when she spotted me.

"No, nothing happened. I just lost track of time."

She gave me a skeptical look, noticing my wet pants, but said nothing.

"We should head back," I said.

An hour later, we were having lunch at the Bar Miramar near the bus station. We watched the fishing boats come into the harbor and the fishermen unload their catch. Helmut and Ingrid showed up in a taxi a few minutes before the bus arrived. They sat together on one of the benches, holding hands and smiling at each other.

We reached Santiago by early evening. Eva and I said goodbye to the German couple. Since Eva had a train to catch, I rode with her in the taxi to the station. We said our goodbyes on the way.

"You've been a good companion on the Camino," she said, giving me a kiss on the cheek. "I'm glad you were here today. It was a nice way to end."

I left the train station and walked up Calle de Hórreo to Rúa das Orfas and into the old city. It was time for me to go home, too. The walk was completed, the sights seen, the prayers made, the apostle hugged, and, after my day in Finisterre, the rituals concluded. I thought I would spend my last day in Santiago exploring the city, buying souvenirs, writing postcards—including one to Michel Mallet, the *hospitalero* in Saint-Jean-Pied-de-Port, to let him know I'd made it to Santiago—and perhaps making one last visit to the cathedral.

I should have known better than to think the Camino was finished with me.

10

HOME

We are never at home, we are always beyond ourselves.
—MICHEL DE MONTAIGNE,
ESSAYS

The Hotel Suso bar was smoky and noisy with students and office workers. I was enjoying a glass of *vino tinto* at a table by the window. Outside it was dark, and the wet cobblestones shone with the light from the shop windows along Ruá do Vilar. Inside, I had my Aurelio Zen novel and a notebook at the ready in case I had a bright idea. After seeing Eva off at the train station and walking back to the old city, it was pleasant to be sitting warm and dry in a bar, watching the street and listening to golden oldies on the bar stereo. I was taking the train to Paris in the morning. I should have been content. Only I wasn't.

I knew it was time to go home. I'd done my Camino. I'd visited Finisterre. It was silly to stay in Santiago any longer. But I didn't want to leave. I wanted to be back on the road. I was finished with the Camino, but I didn't want the Camino to be finished with me. I felt like a branch caught in the backwash of a river current, waiting for something to pull me back into the flow.

The waiter asked if I wanted another glass of wine, breaking the loop of my thoughts. I declined, paid the bill, and left, thinking a long walk would ease my restlessness. I walked up the street to Rúa de Fonseca and across the Praza do Obradoiro. A small crowd stood in front of a statue near the wall of the cathedral. Or at least I thought it was a statue until I got close enough to see a white-faced mime in an ankle-length red cloak standing absolutely motionless on a pedestal. I envied his ability to keep still for so long. I dropped some coins in the hat and gained a wink and a tip of his bowler. The sudden movement made me laugh.

I decided against going into the cathedral. Instead, I walked to Rúa do Pombal and into the park of Carballeira de Santa Susana. I enjoyed the dark, the solitude, and the crunch of gravel beneath my feet as I walked between the twin rows of plane trees. The sound reminded me of the Camino. Light from the lampposts fell through the branches and made the wet tree trunks shine. The noise of the traffic was far away. I sat on a bench and looked up at the stars.

El Camino de las Estrellas, the Way of the Stars; I rolled the phrase around my tongue and tried to imagine what it must have been like for those who lived a thousand years ago to see the Milky Way and be utterly certain that the zodiac, constellations, and planets were influencing human affairs and that the unchanging presence of the stars was evidence of divine order in the cosmos. My mind couldn't— wouldn't?—accept that view of the universe. To me, the stars were gaseous nuclear-powered objects millions of light years away, influencing nothing beyond their gravitational reach.

When it started to rain again, I walked back through the park, following Paseo Santa Susana to where it came out at Avenida de Xoán Carlos. It was noisy with traffic and pedestrians. I passed the lighted windows of the dress shops and hair-dressing salons along Rúa da Senra before cutting up a narrow lane and across the Praza do Toural to Rúa do Vilar. I was back at the Hotel Suso. A young couple holding hands occupied the table where I'd been sitting. I figured I might as well go to my *hospedaje.* Getting drunk wouldn't lessen my restlessness.[1] Better to go to bed, perchance to dream.

But just as I was about to cross the street to my hotel I heard my name. "Hey, Robert! Where are you going? Come back." I turned to see Ron Chanda, the American businessman I'd met two weeks earlier in Carrión de los Condes. He was standing in the doorway of the Hotel Suso. "Come on, have a drink. Henrik's in Santiago, too. I'm waiting for him."

I immediately abandoned my plan to bed down with Aurelio Zen. Once again the Camino, in its serendipitous fashion, was taking care of me. "I'm glad to see you," I said, shaking Ron's hand. "When did you get in?"

"This morning," Ron replied. "With Henrik."

Ron was staying at the same hotel I was, while Henrik the Dane, as I called him, my Camino companion for several days beyond Burgos, was at the Hostal Asa Nova. Ron explained that he and Henrik had met on the Camino before León when Ron, remembering my suggestion to be on the lookout for Henrik, had introduced himself. After that, they'd walked together off and on over the past couple of weeks.

"Did you ever see Andrea again?" I asked, remembering that I'd also introduced him to the Brazilian Bombshell.

"No," he said, "but I'd sure like to. She was something else."

As I followed Ron into the bar and then sat with him at one of the window tables, it struck me that if I'd turned down a different street or gone into another bar, I wouldn't have met him again or be looking forward to an evening with him and Henrik. But then I hadn't even spotted him when I looked in the window at the young couple at my old table. What if Ron hadn't seen me? Was this another of the Camino's gifts of synchronicity?

But the gods, it seemed, were having fun with us this night. Ron and I had just sat down when there was a knocking on the window. We looked up, expecting Henrik. But there was Andrea, blond hair flying and face pressed close to the glass, waving at us. I'll soon be looking everywhere for omens and portents, I thought, as Andrea bounced into the bar to kiss us on each cheek and offer one of her always appreciated hugs. She introduced us to her companion, who was carrying their bags. He was the same guy she had been with in Carrión, but I again forgot his name. Andrea kept up a running patter I couldn't understand, but it hardly mattered. She really was lovely in her flamboyant way; it was a pleasure just to watch her flitting around the room. Tables quickly bunched together, with Andrea as the centerpiece. By the time Henrik arrived, accompanied by an Austrian couple, Peter and Angelique, we had a pilgrim party going.

Henrik and I greeted each other like long-lost brothers, which was perhaps a bit odd considering that we only walked together for a few days. But that was the typical Camino experience: meeting by chance, walking together for a short time, treating each other's blisters if necessary, helping each other, and taking meals together; somehow a sense of intimacy is established, however temporary.

"I'm glad to see you made it," Henrik said. "Your feet are better?"

"Much better." I told him how the pain of walking had suddenly disappeared near Astorga.

"You learned to walk, then. That is good. I wondered if you would." His concern touched me.

Henrik, Ron, Peter, Angelique, and I eventually got up to go out in search of something to eat. All of us were leaving the following morning: Henrik was taking a train to Madrid to catch a plane to Copenhagen; Peter and Angelique were driving back to Vienna; Ron and I, as it turned out, were taking the same train to Hendaye, although he was getting off there to meet friends at Biarritz, and I was changing trains for Paris. Everyone had jobs and families to return to, but we weren't quite ready to put away the scallop shells and walking sticks. The Camino had cast its spell, and we were reluctant to shake it off. We wanted to have a pilgrim meal together. Andrea didn't let us go without another hug, and we were happy to oblige. We left her to her growing flock of admirers.

The five of us wandered along Rúa do Franco past the bars and coffeehouses and restaurants, trying to decide which one to choose. At my suggestion we settled on El Cayado, where I'd dined on my first night in Santiago. It was another wonderful meal. I had the *calamares en su tinta*, baby squid cooked in its own ink, some of the salted Tetilla cheese that is a specialty of Galicia, and glasses of the icy white Ribeira wine. We ended the meal sharing a *tarta de Santiago* and a bottle of almond-flavored Vina Amorina Frangelico.

As we ate and drank we told our stories: blisters in the Navarre, tears on the *meseta*, slogging in El Bierzo, exhaustion in O Cebreiro, relief in Galicia. We compared refugios: Azofra and Rabanal were among the best, with Nájera and Castrojeriz the worst. We related how, somewhere along the Camino, our aches and pains disappeared. As Ron put it, "You got lost in walking." He added, "Sometimes I would be walking along and then look at my watch and find that thirty or forty minutes had gone by without my remembering anything about where I had been walking. I just zoned out."

Everyone had stories of animal encounters, whether with dogs or cows or sheep. I told my tales of the lordly rooster of El Ganso, the dogs of Nájera, and the lizard of Mogarde. I was even sufficiently garrulous to describe my dream about my father and Chonina. To my surprise that prompted a rush of dream recollections from the others. Everyone, it seemed, found that their dreams became more vivid and memorable after a couple of weeks on the Camino.

"It is very difficult for me to live a spiritual life with the everyday stresses, but on the Camino you can allow yourself to feel whole," said Henrik. "The Camino is a place where you feel the presence of God." He continued: "On the Camino, you lose the restraints that keep you disconnected from the things you bury inside and try not to think about because you don't have time to think about them. On the Camino, you have time to remember these things"—he paused, looking at me— "even your dreams."

"It is like a dream," Peter added. "After walking for so long it's hard to believe I have another life, my real life, to go back to."

"I still feel like I'm supposed to be walking," said Ron. "You know it would be a real shame after all the difficulties of the Camino and all that we've discovered if it didn't affect our daily lives."

By the time we'd finished our meal and drawn the conversation to a close, it was past 1 a.m. Since we all had trains to catch in a few hours, we said goodbye to Peter and Angelique outside the restaurant, and then Ron, Henrik, and I walked together to our respective hotels. Ron wanted to go to bed, but Henrik and I decided on one last drink together. We sat at the long bar in the Café de Portugal and ordered brandies. Although we were the only customers, the woman behind the bar didn't seem in any hurry to close. Later we walked to Henrik's hotel and said our goodbyes in the Praza do Toural. After a hug and a handshake, Henrik walked across the square to his hotel, and I walked back to mine. The pilgrimage is well and truly finished, I thought, as I drifted into sleep.

I awoke in the morning to the sound of bells for the last time. It was 6 a.m. I shaved, showered, and dressed in haste. Cinched into my pack, with my walking stick in hand, I stood in the door of my room for one last look. It wasn't much: cracked walls, a creaky bed, a wardrobe that smelled of mothballs, a wobbly lamp on a scarred bedside table, and tall windows that didn't completely close. I tossed the key on the bed, closed the door, and walked down the stairs and out into the rain-shiny streets to the train station on Calle de Hórreo.

Ron was already sitting in the station café when I arrived. So was Charles Henri, whom I'd first met back in Zubiri. It seemed appropriate—another small gift of the Camino?—to end my pilgrimage with someone I'd met at the beginning. He was taking the same train as Ron and I. I asked him how his Camino had been.

"Très content, très content."

Charles explained that he'd arrived in Santiago a few days earlier, but after visiting the cathedral he decided he wanted to walk some more. He took two days to walk back and forth between Santiago and Padrón, a small village about twenty kilometers south of Santiago, where, according to the legend, the boat bearing the body of St. James came ashore. The church there contains a large stone reputed to be the mooring post.

"The city is no place to be for a *peregrino*," Charles said. "You should keep walking."

Aboard the train, Charles sensibly slept in his seat. When the bar car finally opened, Ron and I adjourned there and spent the rest of the trip comfortably ensconced on stools next to a window. "I know we're supposed to be walking," Ron said, "but I'm glad we're not."

We lost track of the bottle count—they were only half-bottles of Rosadas red wine, after all—by the time the train reached León. And somewhere around Pamplona the bartender informed us we'd drained his entire stock. Charles, Ron, and I got off the train in Hendaye to make our respective connections. I said goodbye to Ron and Charles and headed for the 10:45 Palombe Bleue night train to Paris.

Once aboard, I stood by a half-open window in the passageway nursing a coffee as the train rolled through the darkness of the French countryside. I marveled at the warmth of the night air and tried to recollect where I'd been the previous night and the night before that and the week before that. It was all a jumble. I felt homesick, but not for home. I was homesick for the Camino. When I couldn't hold my thoughts together in any coherent way, I returned to my compartment.

The other occupants already had their curtains drawn. I read a few pages of Aurelio Zen's adventures and then fell asleep to the sway and clack of the train. I woke up the next morning to watch the sun come up as the train pulled into Paris.

In hindsight, I realized I had felt a kind of culture shock, a sense of emotional vertigo, at the rapidity of my return to the everyday world and its noisy, blaring distractions. It was disorienting to be sitting on a train watching the land and the sky go by so quickly rather than being part of them as I walked. There was a letdown, a sense of deflation, as the train crossed in a few hours the same terrain that had taken me more than a month to cover on foot. Sitting in the bar with Ron, watching the country roll past, the greenery of Galicia giving way to the mountains and the *meseta* and the rolling fields of Navarre turning into the forests of the Pyrenees, I felt as though I was waking from a long dream, crossing back over a threshold from a realm of enchantment to the world of disenchantment.

I stayed in touch with Henrik and Ron for a time. It seemed they felt the same as I did. Henrik sent me pictures from the Camino and a letter. "I hold this Camino as a jewel in my heart," he wrote. "It was good, and I want to do it again." Ron needed physiotherapy for his Achilles tendons, but he was soon walking the Camino again, taking in several portions that he'd previously missed, as well as parts of the route through Portugal.

The real gift of the Camino, the one that has lingered with me over the years since my pilgrimage, was to have found a place I could return to imaginatively over and over, recreating that heightened awareness of the world. It was as though my pilgrimage had been a preparation for other journeys, both inward and outward—an initiation into a practice that would allow me to sharpen and deepen my pilgrim sensibility, whether I was on the road or not. Out of the blue I would catch myself remembering solitary conversations with my father or those singular moments when, by the alchemy of solitude and silence and the steady rhythm of walking, I felt myself disappear. And even though the immediacy of my Camino experience eventually faded, there would be times—walking to work in the morning, sitting in the living room late at night when the house was quiet, strolling through a park—when images of a green path or the vault of the sky or the dim interior of a church or a splash of yellow paint on a rock rose sharp in my mind. For a few seconds, I was on the Camino again, a pilgrim again, journeying through a realm both beyond and within myself.[2]

EPILOGUE

*Old things are past away, all's become
new.
Strange! he's another man.*

—JOHN BUNYAN,
THE PILGRIM'S PROGRESS

On a fine sunny day in late May, I was walking out of Santiago de
Compostela to meet my son as he completed his first pilgrimage. I ambled through the Porto do Camiño and followed the road beyond the
old city. Eight years earlier, I'd stumbled along these same streets as I
came into Santiago on the last day of my first pilgrimage. But that was
then and this was now.

Daniel and I had started out together a month earlier at Saint-Jean-
Pied-de-Port, climbing the Pyrenees over the Napoleon Route into
Roncesvalles. But eventually I decided I didn't want to walk the whole
route again. I put away my *credencial*, renounced my status as a pilgrim,
and became a tourist. I contented myself with walking a few days at
a time and then taking a bus or a train across those stretches of the
Camino I wasn't interested in repeating. Daniel, however, wanted to
walk as much of the route as he could. As a result, I often found myself in some town two or three days ahead of him. With cell phones
and e-mail, technologies that hadn't been available on my first pilgrimage, it was easy to stay in touch and arrange to meet. So while he did
the hard slogging, I spent my time exploring places—Logroño, Burgos,
León—that I'd only passed through before. I also thought a bit about
the Camino and what it had come to mean to me.

We all possess a spiritual life to one degree or another—a moral inwardness informed by religious sentiment (or lack thereof), intellectual concepts, and opinions rooted in experience. I've heard it said that the mark of sanity in the modern world is the ability to hold as many contradictory notions in your head as you can at one time and still keep functioning. If that's true, and I think it is, then it's surely a bid for sanity to seek a time and a place to reflect on the spiritual dimension of our lives, in a way that might help us keep a grip on the contradictions. Many people seem willing to forego this effort, apparently content with the diversions of consumption and entertainment offered nowadays. But others feel a compelling need for something more. The difficulty, however, is a matter not only of learning the habits of reflection and the skills of introspection that can help us discover what "more" there might be, but also of finding the time, the place, and the circumstances that make it possible for us to reflect on our deepest cares and concerns.[1]

I was lucky. I had stumbled onto pilgrimage. I found not only a practice but also a time, a place, and a set of circumstances that allowed me to retreat temporarily from the modern world and to foster a more reflective mindset. In this regard, I can agree with the scholar George Greenia, a professor of modern languages at the College of William & Mary, about the value of pilgrimage. "I am now a true believer in time invested outside of our professional and familial routines," he writes. "Well used as a corrective to our usual mindless trotting around, these interludes [of pilgrimage] can get us to stride past our accustomed selves. The journey forces us into silence, makes us put down our books, abandon our computers, and may lead us to a disciplined re-imagining of the life and habits of another age."[2]

Deep down I had wanted my pilgrimage to confront my disbelief and reveal the divine, but it was not to be. Ian Bradley sums up this longing well: "The desire to be pilgrims perhaps reflects yearnings to find a deeper purpose and sense of rest. It also chimes with the way that increasing numbers of people describe their faith as an ongoing journey rather than a sudden decisive conversion experience."[3] To be sure, I had gained no sudden spiritual transformation on my Camino.[4] But that was probably as it should be. As the anthropologist Alan Morinis observes, "While the sacred place may be the source of spiritual enlightenment, it is at home once again that the effect of that enlightenment and what salvation has been gained is confirmed. The return journey and the re-incorporation of the pilgrim into social life are the test of the pilgrimage. Has there been change? Will it last?"[5]

In the months after my return, restored to the routines and habits of job and family, I did become aware of subtle shifts in myself, changes not so much in behavior but in perception. I felt more content with everyday pleasures—sitting in the back yard admiring my wife's garden creations, for example—instead of feeling that something important was going on elsewhere and I was missing it. My ordinary world was more extraordinary, more enchanted in its everydayness.

I certainly didn't feel this way all the time. Modern life is too hectic and demanding to leave you in peace or to allow general equanimity. Still, I noticed myself deliberately pausing and consciously paying attention to the world around me. It's not that I avoided long hours at work or the responsibilities of daily life. But more and more frequently I found myself taking long solitary walks, something I had seldom done before my pilgrimage. I imagined myself back on the Camino, attempting to maintain my pilgrimage mindset. In this fashion I was able to retain one of the great gifts of the Camino: the ability to slow down physically in order to slow down mentally. I had indeed learned to walk and would embark on other pilgrimages as well.[6]

On the pilgrimage with my son, although I abandoned my pilgrim status, I could still on occasion lose myself in the walking—in "zoning out," to borrow Ron Chanda's phrase. Even in the cities, it was possible to disappear. While I waited for Daniel in Santiago, I wandered the streets, looking into nooks and crannies I hadn't seen the first time. I went to the cathedral to hug the statue of St. James and to pray for everyone I could remember—Chonina, I thought, would be a teenager now—and I sat in a pew during Mass while the great silver *botafumeiro* swung over the crowd, trailing clouds of incense. I discovered a solitary cherry tree in a small cobblestone square, where I sat on a bench and watched the petals fall until it sometimes seemed that I was falling, too. Between the walking and the churchgoing and the blossom-viewing, I could disappear for hours.

It was in that frame of mind that I waited for my son while sitting on a park bench beneath a palm tree in one of Santiago's suburbs. We'd talked on our cell phones earlier, and I knew the route he would take, walking in from Monte del Gozo. But I wasn't sure what time he'd arrive. It didn't matter. I was content to enjoy the passing pedestrians and to read through James Michener's *Iberia*, a copy of which I'd bought a couple of days earlier in a Santiago bookstore. I had carried the book with me when I hitchhiked across Spain and Portugal in the 1970s. Now rereading Michener's descriptions of his pilgrimage on the Camino de Santiago filled me with a sudden longing for a whole series of concurrent lives in which I could simultaneously relive my past even as I lived my present. Why hadn't it occurred to me to walk the Camino three decades ago? I was certainly in better shape physically when I was thirty years younger. But what spiritual inclinations did I have back then, if any? Was it possible, though, that Michener's book had planted the seed for a pilgrimage and it had lain dormant all these years, waiting for the right season and a fertile psyche?

I closed the book and looked up the road in the direction from which Daniel would come. I thought I could see a familiar figure in the distance. I squinted, but it was gone. Then it was back, reappearing as it climbed a slope in the road. I could make out the red jacket, the hump of the backpack, and the walking stick. I saw my son clearly now in the morning light. I'd know that tall, long-legged stride anywhere, and I felt an aching pride as his father.

Then I had the strangest sensation: even as I watched Daniel coming toward me there was a brief moment when, by some trick of light and longing, I was looking at a younger version of myself.

NOTES

PROLOGUE

1. Nolan and Nolan, *Christian Pilgrimage in Modern Western Europe*, 1–2.

2. Iyer, foreword to *Traveling Souls*, ix.

3. One book of particular value is *The Pilgrimage Road to Santiago: The Complete Cultural Handbook* by David M. Gitlitz and Linda Kay Davidson. A more recent guidebook is Jaffa Raza's *The Village to Village Guide to the Camino Santiago*. Books about the Camino experience are increasingly popular, but I still prefer the older ones that inspired me. They include Edward F. Stanton's *Road of Stars to Santiago*, Lee Hoinacki's *El Camino: Walking to Santiago de Compostela*, Walter Starkie's *The Road to Santiago: Pilgrims of St. James*, Edwin Mullins's *The Pilgrimage to Santiago*, and Elyn Aviva's *Following the Milky Way: A Pilgrimage on the Camino de Santiago*. Some of the more recent books I've enjoyed include Conrad Rudolph's *Pilgrimage to the End of the World: The Road to Santiago de Compostela*, Rosanne Keller's *Pilgrim in Time*, Arthur Paul Boers's *The Way Is Made by Walking: A Pilgrimage Along the Camino de Santiago*, Joyce Rupp's *Walk in a Relaxed Manner: Life Lessons from the Camino*, Guy Thatcher's *A Journey of Days: Relearning Life's Lessons on the Camino de Santiago*, and Ian Bradley's *Pilgrimage: A Spiritual and Cultural Journey*.

I. PRAYER

1. In terms of literal accuracy, my remembrance of what Lewis said was shaky at the time but not, I think, spiritually inaccurate. Tracking the source of my recollection when I returned home, I found that in *Mere Christianity* Lewis describes faith as a "necessary virtue" that requires discipline and practice lest it fade:

> Consequently, one must train the habit of Faith. . . . The first step is to recognize the fact that your moods change. The next is to make sure that, if you have once accepted Christianity, then some of its main doctrines shall be deliberately held before your mind for some time every day. That is why daily prayers and religious readings and churchgoing are necessary parts of the Christian life. We have to be continually reminded of what we believe. Neither this belief nor any other will automatically remain alive to the mind. It must be fed. (140–41)

2. Eliot, "Little Gidding," section 1, lines 47–48, in *Four Quartets*.

3. I have borrowed my etymological understanding from Cousineau, *The Art of Pilgrimage*, 13–14; and Hitt, *Off the Road*, 51.

4. For personal pilgrimage accounts, see Hoinacki's *El Camino*, Starkie's *The Road to Santiago*, and Mullins's *The Pilgrimage to Santiago*. For books that explore the *idea* of pilgrimage, see especially *Pilgrim Stories: On and Off the Road to Santiago* by Nancy Louise Frey; *Traveling Souls: Contemporary Pilgrimage Stories*, edited by Brian Bouldrey; and Cousineau's *The Art of Pilgrimage*.

5. Stanton, *Road of Stars to Santiago*, 83. I have also taken the Talmud epigraph at the beginning of this chapter from Stanton's book.

6. In addition to the sources mentioned in note 4, Mary Jo Anderson's brief but comprehensive essay summarizing the history and legends of the Camino, "Pilgrimage to the Stars," contributed much to my knowledge. She walked the Camino in 1999.

7. Gitlitz and Davidson write, "Relics were very important to medieval Catholics, who believed that some of the aura of divinity associated with Christ or the saints remained in their bones, or in the objects associated with them." Venerating these relics "put the worshiper in direct contact with the divine." *The Pilgrimage Road to Santiago*, 61.

8. Sumption, *Pilgrimage*, 114.

9. Mullins quotes an 1845 book by the British travel writer Richard Ford, *A Handbook for Travellers*: "Pilgrimage, the oriental and medieval form of traveling, is passing away even in Spain. The carcass remains, but the spirit is fled." *The Pilgrimage to Santiago*, 55.

10. MacLaine, *The Camino*.

11. Iyer, foreword to *Traveling Souls*, ix.

12. Ibid., vii.

13. Starkie quotes a medieval English pilgrim, Andrew Broode: "As to wine, it doth actuate and doth quicken a man's wits, it doth comfort the heart, it doth scour the liver." *The Road to Santiago*, 6.

14. Eco, *Travels in Hyperreality*, 64–65. It is worth quoting Eco more fully on this point: "The Middle Ages are the root of all our contemporary 'hot' problems, and it is not surprising that we go back to that period every time we ask ourselves about our origins."

2. PAIN

1. Stanton, *Road of Stars to Santiago*, 21–22.

2. Cees Nooteboom quotes Picaud: "The people of Navarre are full of malice, swarthy of complexion, ugly of appearance, depraved, perverse, despicable, disloyal, corrupt, lechers, drunkards and past masters of all forms of violence, wild, savage, treacherous, deceitful, blasphemous and foul-mannered, cruel and quarrelsome, incapable of honorable behavior. All vices come easily to them." *Roads to Santiago*, 323–24. Mullins also extracts a similar description from Picaud's *Codex Calixtinus*. *The Pilgrimage to Santiago*, 127.

3. Many writers about the Camino convey Picaud's commentary. See Starkie, *The Road to Santiago*, 138–39; Hoinacki, *El Camino*, 15–19; Mullins, *The Pilgrimage to Santiago*, 126–27; and Hitt, *Off the Road*, 63.

4. See Starkie, *The Road to Santiago*, 21–22; Mullins, *The Pilgrimage to Santiago*, 7–8, 33, 116–27; Frey, *Pilgrim Stories*, 8–14; Anderson, "Pilgrimage to the Stars"; and Hitt, *Off the Road*, 56–57, 61.

5. See Mullins, *The Pilgrimage to Santiago*, 122–23; and Hoinacki, *El Camino*, 8–9.

6. Cited in Mullins, *The Pilgrimage to Santiago*, 125; and Starkie, *The Road to Santiago*, 40.

7. See Starkie, *The Road to Santiago*, 21–22; Mullins, *The Pilgrimage to Santiago*, 7–8; Frey, *Pilgrim Stories*, 8–14; and Anderson, "Pilgrimage to the Stars."

8. Hoinacki expresses this as "faith in the thamaturgical powers of relics." *El Camino*, 26.

9. As Nooteboom observes, "It is necessary to separate medieval man from the comfortable romantic images we have formed of him. . . . He was a truly different human being, with different preoccupations. His society was a spiritual unity; the importance that he attached to the relics of saints and martyrs is beyond modern comprehension. Seeking out and venerating those sacred reliquaries, devoted Christians tramped from country to country, from shrine to shrine, an inspired multitude of prayerful, lifelong travelers." *Roads to Santiago*, 50.

10. See Starkie, *The Road to Santiago*, 22–23: "The discovery of the relics of St. James caused a sensation, not only throughout western Christendom, but also throughout Islam. It brought consolation and hope to Europe that the triumphant progress of Mohammedanism would be checked."

11. Cited in Hitt, *Off the Road*, 37–38. See also Mullins, *The Pilgrimage to Santiago*, 9–10, 12. Mullins suggests that the idea of St. James being buried in northern Spain may be the result of a mistranslation of Greek texts into Latin. The Greek documents refer to St. James being buried at Anchaion in Marmarica, a Roman province in northern Africa near the Nile Delta, which, says Mullins, seems feasible. But in the translation from Greek to Latin, Anchaion in Marmarica appears as *in arca marmorica*—or "in a marble tomb." Mullins, *The Pilgrimage to Santiago*, 7–8.

12. See Starkie, *The Road to Santiago*, 23–24.

13. See Mullins, *The Pilgrimage to Santiago*, 32–34. He makes an interesting observation: "It is food for thought what might have happened to Europe and to Christianity had the Arabs not been stopped, and stopped soon. London might be as Moorish as Baghdad, and the *Koran* be read in Canterbury." Lest anyone think I've cast Islam too darkly and been too easy on Christianity's bloody history, it is well to remember that until the Moorish invasions of Spain, the Christian church was not overly militant. As Mullins states, "It was Islam that taught European rulers the notion of a 'holy war,' and taught European churchmen the binding power of moral propaganda. Both were central to the spirit of pilgrimage."

14. See Starkie, *The Road to Santiago*, 37, 69. Anderson, in "Pilgrimage to the Stars," quotes the song:

Tallifer who was famed for song
Mounted on a charger strong,
Rode on before the Duke and sang
Of Roland and Charlemagne,
Of Oliver and the vassals all
Who fell in fight at Roncesvalles.

15. Mullins, *The Pilgrimage to Santiago*, 22.

16. I owe this reference to *Hamlet* to Starkie, *The Road to Santiago*, 60; see also Anderson, "Pilgrimage to the Stars."

17. Aviva refers to Sir Walter Raleigh's poem in *Following the Milky Way*, 107.

18. Anderson makes this observation regarding painters' references to St. James in "Pilgrimage to the Stars."

19. Nooteboom writes that the Camino de Santiago "is one of the arias of madness of European opera, a gigantic migratory flow, a movement of millions of extras, an unceasing stream of scallop-bearing pilgrims from all corners of Christendom." *Roads to Santiago*, 200. Anderson writes that as the millions of pilgrims tramped the Camino, "they exchanged ideas about architecture, fashion, ballads, politics, food, and philosophy," all of which helped forge a sense of European identity. "Pilgrimage to the Stars."

20. Starkie, *The Road to Santiago*, 1.

3. PATHS

1. I owe my surgery skills to Stanton, *Road of Stars to Santiago*, 29–30. I should note, however, that he had friends do the job, and they used alcohol instead of iodine. I have no idea if that makes any difference in terms of the shrieking.

2. Starkie, *The Road to Santiago*, 6.

3. On the idea of *communitas*, see Frey, *Pilgrim Stories*, 92–99, 226–27. I would be remiss in not acknowledging how much I benefited from Frey's wide-ranging, insightful, and informative study, both in preparing for my pilgrimage and in understanding it afterward. Her influence is woven through my narrative.

4. Quoted by Mullins, *The Pilgrimage to Santiago*, 136.

5. Starkie relayed this phrase in *The Road to Santiago*, 194.

6. My English version of the Blessing is based on a multilingual brochure I found in the church.

7. Starkie, *The Road to Santiago*, 140.

8. Frey, *Pilgrim Stories*, 50–52, 125–36.

4. TIME

1. Stanton experienced a similar sense of timelessness. See *Road of Stars to Santiago*, 68. See also Frey, *Pilgrim Stories*, 81–82. It is worth quoting Frey on this phenomenon: "With the change in linear, directional time, pilgrims often sense that time blends and folds together: past, present, and future coexist. Pilgrims commonly experience themselves with pilgrims of the past as they walk, rest, take shelter, drink at a fountain, cross a bridge, pray in a church."

2. Coelho, *The Pilgrimage*, 253.

3. My Spanish wasn't that good and my Dutch nonexistent, so I've had to rely on Cees Nooteboom's translation. He noticed the memorial when he drove through Navarrete on one of his many tours of Spain. See *Roads to Santiago*, 326.

4. Frey, *Pilgrim Stories*, 84.

5. Hitt, *Off the Road*, 108–11.

6. In *Pilgrim Stories*, 106–8, Frey observes that contemporary experiences of dogs on the Camino are "tame" compared to what medieval pilgrims endured, but would-be pilgrims still feel anxious about potential encounters.

7. MacLaine, *The Camino*, 170.

8. My experience was not unusual. Long-distance walking has psychological by-products. Hitt describes a "hallucinatory open house" of shopping mall Muzak, Christmas carols, Top 40 hits, and conversations with ex-girlfriends and his mother as he walked. *Off the Road*, 108. Likewise, Stanton writes, "There's something about the act of walking, its rhythm nudges the memory, brings words, phrases, verses, songs to consciousness." *Road of Stars to Santiago*, 54.

9. Those songs—"From a Jack to a King," "The Night Has a Thousand Eyes," and "Moon River"—were sung, respectively, by Ned Miller, Bobby Vee, and Pat Boone, so far as I recall. Readers may notice that I somewhat misremembered the lines from Miller's song.

10. The lines, now rendered accurately instead of what I had scribbled down at the time, are from, respectively, Matthew Arnold's "To Marguerite," John Milton's *Paradise Lost*, and T. S. Eliot's "Little Gidding" in *Four Quartets*.

11. Frey, *Pilgrim Stories*, 82–83.

12. Ibid., 45. Frey refers to this therapeutic dimension of the Camino.

13. Larkin, *Collected Poems*, 97–98.

5. GRATITUDE

1. Frey devotes a section of her study to psychological phenomena of the pilgrimage such as these. See *Pilgrim Stories*, 72–81.

2. For the exact lines, see Thomas, "Kneeling," *Collected Poems*, 199.

3. Frey writes, "For many, the Camino exists outside of normal time in neutral and inspiring places, where stress is reduced to a minimum. In this environment pilgrims open up internally and externally to those around them." *Pilgrim Stories*, 101.

4. Ibid., 113.

5. Stanton, *Road of Stars to Santiago*, 88.

6. GIFTS

1. Stanton, *Road of Stars to Santiago*, 136; Gitlitz and Davidson, *The Pilgrimage Road to Santiago*, 277; Aviva, *Following the Milky Way*, 193–94; and Facaros and Pauls, *Northern Spain*, 239–40.

2. Facaros and Pauls, *Northern Spain*, 240.

3. Stanton describes this part of the Camino, with its half-abandoned villages, this

way: "Everything seems unreal, a dream of what happened long ago." *Road of Stars to Santiago*, 136.

4. Aviva offers a brief history of the Cruz de Ferro. See *Following the Milky Way*, 199–200. See also Gitlitz and Davidson, *The Pilgrimage Road to Santiago*, 284.

5. See R. S. Thomas, "Ap Huw's Testament," in *Collected Poems*, 83.

6. See Hitt, *Off the Road*, 193.

7. Ibid., 190. Hitt's description of the ritual is more sardonic—and more hilarious—than mine.

7. VISIONS

1. See Mullins, *The Pilgrimage to Santiago*, 192–93; Aviva, *Following the Milky Way*, 224–25; and Gitlitz and Davidson, *The Pilgrimage Road to Santiago*, 304–7.

2. Frey writes that "pilgrims report the experience of arrival in O Cebreiro as a shift to another time and stage of the Camino. Within this environment pilgrims experience many of these changes on the internal level as well. O Cebreiro is often a point where stories of visions and insight surface after the physical trial is overcome." *Pilgrim Stories*, 141.

3. See Hoinacki, *El Camino*, 214–15; Starkie, *The Road to Santiago*, 292–93; Gitlitz and Davidson, *The Pilgrimage Road to Santiago*, 304–5; and Aviva, *Following the Milky Way*, 225. I must also mention that the Church of Santa María la Real is the resting place of the parish priest Don Elías Valiña Sampedro, who was instrumental in ensuring the restoration and preservation of O Cebreiro's buildings, including the Hostal San Giraldo de Aurillac.

4. See the evocative description by Michener in *Iberia*, 889–90: "Starving soldiers had to listen impotently as the worthless gold clinked down the mountainside.... Soldiers would lie down in the ditch, a bottle of wine to their lips, knowing that if they got drunk they would not rise again, but they drank on and hundreds made the noiseless transition from drunkenness to death." See also Facaros and Pauls, *Northern Spain*, 252.

5. Aviva, *Following the Milky Way*, 229. She writes that the able-bodied received "firewood, salt and water and two blankets," while the sick enjoyed "bread, eggs and lard."

6. See Mullins, *The Pilgrimage to Santiago*, 194. He quotes Picaud's *Codex Calixtinus* as saying the region lacked good wine, but possessed ample supplies of "rye bread, cider, milk, honey and enormous river fish."

7. Gitlitz and Davidson, *The Pilgrimage Road to Santiago*, 304.

8. Aviva, *Following the Milky Way*, 103. She makes a similar observation about the sensory intensity of the Camino experience. "Every moment on the Camino was filled with experience, intense awareness of my feet, my shoulders, the ground, the sun, hunger, pain, thirst, friendship, accomplishment, exhaustion."

9. Cousineau, *The Art of Pilgrimage*, 14–15.

10. Iyer, foreword to *Traveling Souls*, xi.

11. See Cousineau, *The Art of Pilgrimage*, xxiv–xxv and 13–15; Iyer, foreword to *Traveling Souls*, ix–xi; and Westwood, *Sacred Journeys*, 10–15.

12. Stanton, *Road of Stars to Santiago*, 54–55.

13. Quoted in Iyer, foreword to *Traveling Souls*, xi.

14. Victor and Edith Turner, *Image and Pilgrimage in Christian Culture*; see especially chapter 1.

15. Eliot, "Litle Gidding," section 1, lines 32–34, in *Four Quartets*.

8. UNDERGLIMMER

1. This deepening sensory awareness was not uncommon. Frey points out that pilgrims often develop an intense sense of place as they walk. She refers to one pilgrim who found it "possible to see individual blades of grass, feel every stone in the road (maybe painfully), and note how the senses are heightened." *Pilgrim Stories*, 74–75.

2. Iyer writes, "The pilgrim, like any traveler, is mostly traveling inside herself, to a destination not found on any map." Foreword to *Traveling Souls*, ix.

3. This translation of Bashō's poem is from Dorothy Britton's *A Haiku Journey: Bashō's Narrow Road to a Far Province*, 62. The "underglimmer" phrase is attributed to Bashō by Cousineau in *The Art of Pilgrimage*, xix.

4. Frey notes that it's not uncommon for modern-day pilgrims to "experience themselves with pilgrims of the past as they walk. . . . Some modern pilgrims feel their presence strongly." *Pilgrim Stories*, 81–82.

5. Frey points out that "while journeying through this different time and place pilgrims find that long-forgotten memories surface; memories of family members and friends, childhood places, secrets or painful circumstances. . . . Into these quiet moments may spill unexpected tears." Ibid., 82–83.

6. Hoinacki seems to have had a similar experience. "The pain, mud, and a month's walking have brought me to a new place. . . . I feel that the exercise and pain have allowed me to enter this place through a full, sensory involvement; my senses have made me into a being of fine and delicate awareness. I am—for me—a new kind of rational sensorium." *El Camino*, 259–60.

7. Starkie quotes Domenico Laffi, an Italian who walked from Bologna to Santiago in the seventeenth century and who described the sight from Monte del Gozo: "We could see the longed-for and often-mentioned Santiago, about half a league away, appearing so suddenly that we fell on our knees, the excess of joy bringing tears to our eyes. We began to sing the *Te Deum*." *The Road to Santiago*, 305–6.

8. In referring to "Porto do Camiño" I should explain that when you enter Galicia, you see signs in Gallego, the Galician language, which differs in some respects from Spanish. Signs and street names are occasionally given in both languages.

9. DISAPPEARANCE

1. Quoted in Hitt, *Off the Road*, 246. The further comments by García Márquez about the square in Santiago are also worth quoting: "Its poise and its youthful air prohibit you from even thinking about its venerable age; instead, it looks as if it had been

built the day before by someone who had lost their sense of time." Indeed, the huge square and the buildings that surround it span the history of Western architecture: a Romanesque religious college; the Renaissance Hostal de los Reyes Católicos, built in the early 1500s by King Ferdinand and Queen Isabella as a pilgrim hospital but now a five-star *parador*; the eighteenth-century neoclassical Concello de Santiago, the local city hall; and, of course, the baroque cathedral itself.

2. See Frey, *Pilgrim Stories*, 146, 155, 164–65. She writes that arrival in Santiago "often comes as an unpleasant surprise as the joy of discovery comes to a sudden halt." Pilgrims, she says, "describe both a sense of elation at having reached the goal . . . and despondency at seeing the experience come to an end. . . . After growing accustomed to walking or cycling for five to eight hours a day the sudden change produces a shock to the body now inhibited from maintaining its daily rhythm." See also Hoinacki, *El Camino*, 273. He describes his puzzled ambivalence toward his arrival in Santiago as a spell of "depression" and laments that he "will not gaze at a horizon, knowing that just on the other side, an ever new vision of creation awaits [him]."

3. The sentiment is not unusual. As I've already pointed out in chapter 4, Coelho says something similar. Likewise, Stanton writes, "My body seemed to walk itself, the road walking my body." *Road of Stars to Santiago*, 192.

4. Thomas, "Kneeling," *Collected Poems*, 199. Devotees of Thomas's poetry will recognize that I wasn't word-for-word accurate in what I remembered at the time.

5. Mullins, *The Pilgrimage to Santiago*, 199; and Starkie, *The Road to Santiago*, 308.

6. Aviva, *Following the Milky Way*, 259; and Hitt, *Off the Road*, 247–48.

7. Gitlitz and Davidson, *The Pilgrimage Road to Santiago*, 352–53.

8. Starkie, *The Road to Santiago*, 312.

9. Stanton noticed a similar diminishment of interest in sex during his pilgrimage. *Road of Stars to Santiago*, 113, 173. That doesn't seem to be the case for everyone, however, judging from the reactions to the Brazilian Bombshell, for example. Indeed, as Frey recounts, love affairs along the Camino are not unusual. She observes that many pilgrims feel an increase in sexual energy, due in large part to the decrease in stress: "In the anonymous, open environment of the pilgrimage relationships of a temporary nature as well as romances that continue after the Camino are not uncommon." *Pilgrim Stories*, 115–17.

10. Frey, *Pilgrim Stories*, 171–76.

11. See Stanton, *Road of Stars to Santiago*, 193; and Frey, *Pilgrim Stories*, 174. Frey writes that Finisterre provides "a point of symbolic death and rebirth, or destruction and resurrection."

12. For the exact wording, see Thomas, "The Other," *Collected Poems*, 457. I didn't of course remember it letter-perfect at the time, but I got the spirit of it.

10. HOME

1. Frey points out that post-pilgrimage extremes in behavior are common among pilgrims. Symptoms include excessive drinking and revelry and a compulsion to walk the streets. *Pilgrim Stories*, 164.

2. Again, Frey notes that after returning home, "pilgrims do not just remember the Camino, they often speak of going back with their senses and feeling as if they are on the road again." The initial pilgrimage, she writes, "may be just the beginning of a much longer series of inner journeys in which the participant retains the feeling of being a pilgrim even though he or she is not on the road." Ibid., 224–26.

EPILOGUE

1. I have long been haunted by an essay on Marcel Proust's *À la recherche du temps perdu* by the German writer Walter Benjamin, for whom Proust was "filled with the insight that none of us has the time to live the true dramas of the life that we are destined for." Quoted in Berger, *Selected Essays*, 188.

2. George Greenia, "Pilgrimage as Therapy."

3. Bradley, *Pilgrimage*, 20.

4. I wasn't unique in this lack of revelation. Stanton writes, "Of course I have not been transformed as I dreamed. I should have foreseen that no pilgrimage, no single journey or act suffices." *Road of Stars to Santiago*, 192.

5. Quoted in Frey, *Pilgrim Stories*, 178.

6. The inspiration of the Camino and a subsequent pilgrimage to Japan eventually prompted me to write a book about paying attention and the experiences of everyday mysticism. See *A Rumour of God: Rekindling Belief in an Age of Disenchantment*.

BIBLIOGRAPHY

Anderson, Mary Jo. "Pilgrimage to the Stars." *Crisis*, February 2000.

Aviva, Elyn. *Following the Milky Way: A Pilgrimage on the Camino de Santiago*. Ames: Iowa State University Press, 1989.

Berger, John. *Selected Essays*. Edited by Geoff Dyer. New York: Random House, 2001.

Boers, Arthur Paul. *The Way Is Made by Walking: A Pilgrimage Along the Camino de Santiago*. Madison, WI: InterVarsity Press, 2007.

Bouldrey, Brian, ed. *Traveling Souls: Contemporary Pilgrimage Stories*. San Francisco: Whereabouts Press, 1999.

Bradley, Ian. *Pilgrimage: A Spiritual and Cultural Journey*. Oxford: Lion Hudson, 2009.

Britton, Dorothy. *A Haiku Journey: Bashō's Narrow Road to a Far Province*. New York: Kodansha International, 1974.

Carson, Anne. *Plainwater: Essays and Poetry*. New York: Vintage Contemporaries, 1995.

Coelho, Paulo. *The Pilgrimage: A Contemporary Quest for Ancient Wisdom*. New York: Harper Collins, 1997.

Cousineau, Phil. *The Art of Pilgrimage: The Seeker's Guide to Making Travel Sacred*. Berkeley: Conari Press, 1998.

Eco, Umberto. *Travels in Hyperreality*. New York: Harcourt Brace & Company, 1986.

Eliot, T. S. *Four Quartets*. London: Faber and Faber, 1944.

Facaros, Dana, and Michael Pauls. *Northern Spain*. London: Cadogan Guides, 1999.

Frey, Nancy Louise. *Pilgrim Stories: On and Off the Road to Santiago*. Berkeley: University of California Press, 1998.

Gitlitz, David M., and Linda Kay Davidson. *The Pilgrimage Road to Santiago: The Complete Cultural Handbook*. New York: St. Martin's Griffin, 2000.

Gower, Kathy. "Incorporating a Hero's Journey: A Modern Day Pilgrimage on the Camino de Santiago." Ph.D. diss., California Institute of Integral Studies, 2002.

Greenia, George. "Pilgrimage as Therapy." *W & M News*, September 22, 2005.

Harrison, Kathryn. *The Road to Santiago*. Washington, DC: National Geographic Society, 2003.

Hitt, Jack. *Off the Road: A Modern-Day Walk Down the Pilgrim's Route into Spain.* New York: Simon & Schuster, 1994.

Hoinacki, Lee. *El Camino: Walking to Santiago de Compostela.* University Park: Pennsylvania State University Press, 1996.

Iyer, Pico. Foreword to *Traveling Souls: Contemporary Pilgrimage Stories.* Edited by Brian Bouldrey. San Francisco: Whereabouts Press, 1999.

Keller, Rosanne. *Pilgrim in Time.* Collegeville, MN: Liturgical Press, 2006.

Larkin, Philip. *Collected Poems.* New York: Faber and Faber, 1988.

Lewis, C. S. *Mere Christianity.* San Francisco: Harper, [1943] 2001.

MacLaine, Shirley. *The Camino: A Journey of the Spirit.* New York: Simon & Schuster, 2000.

Mahoney, Rosemary. *The Singular Pilgrim.* Boston: Houghton Mifflin Company, 2003.

Melczer, William. *The Pilgrim's Guide to Santiago de Compostela.* New York: Ithaca Press, 1993.

Michener, James. *Iberia: Spanish Travels and Reflections.* New York: Random House, [1968] 1984.

Mullins, Edwin. *The Pilgrimage to Santiago.* New York: E. P. Dutton & Company, 1957.

Niebuhr, Richard R. "Pilgrims and Pioneers." *Parabola* 9, no. 3 (1984): 6–13.

Nolan, Mary Lee, and Sidney Nolan. *Christian Pilgrimage in Modern Western Europe.* Chapel Hill: University of North Carolina Press, 1989.

Nooteboom, Cees. *Roads to Santiago: A Modern-Day Pilgrimage through Spain.* Translated from the Dutch by Ina Rilke. New York: Harcourt, 1992.

Raza, Jaffa. *The Village to Village Guide to the Camino Santiago.* 2nd ed. London: Simon Wallenburg Press, 2007.

Rudolph, Conrad. *Pilgrimage to the End of the World: The Road to Santiago de Compostela.* Chicago: University of Chicago Press, 2004.

Rupp, Joyce. *Walk in a Relaxed Manner: Life Lessons from the Camino.* Maryknoll, NY: Orbis Books, 2007.

Sibley, Robert. *A Rumour of God: Rekindling Belief in an Age of Disenchantment.* Toronto: Novalis, 2010.

Stanton, Edward F. *Road of Stars to Santiago.* Lexington: University Press of Kentucky, 1994.

Starkie, Walter. *The Road to Santiago: Pilgrims of St. James.* New York: E. P. Dutton & Company, 1957.

Sumption, Jonathan. *Pilgrimage: An Image of Medieval Religion.* London: Faber and Faber, 1975.

Thatcher, Guy. *A Journey of Days: Relearning Life's Lessons on the Camino de Santiago.* Renfrew, Ontario: General Store Publishing House, 2008.

Thomas, R. S. *Collected Poems: 1945–1990.* London: Phoenix, 1993.

Turner, Victor, and Edith Turner. *Image and Pilgrimage in Christian Culture: Anthropological Perspectives.* New York: Columbia University Press, 1978.

Ward, Robert. *All the Good Pilgrims: Tales of the Camino de Santiago.* Toronto: Thomas Allen, 2007.

Westwood, Jennifer. *Sacred Journeys: An Illustrated Guide to Pilgrimages around the World.* New York: Henry Holt, 1997.

INDEX

Lopos, Andrea Libia, 51, 78, 79, 128,
143–44
Los Arcos, 53–54

Machado, Antonio, 42
Machiavelli, Niccoló, 54
MacLaine, Shirley, 15, 17, 36, 60, 61, 92
Mallet, Michel, 17, 39, 64, 140
Maragatos, 84, 85
Márquez, Gabriel García, 126, 159–60n1
(chap. 9)
Muruzábal, 48
Merton, Thomas, 17
Melide, 120
meseta (Tierra de Campos), 71, 74, 75, 78,
128, 144, 147
Michener, James, 152, 158n4 (chap. 7)
Milton, John, 63
Molinaseca, 91, 92, 136
Montaigne, Michel de, 97, 141
Monte del Gozo, 123–24
Mooney, Kerri, 48–50
Morgade, 131
Morinis, Alain, 150
Moses, 109, 133
Mullins, Edwin, 155n11, 155n13
Murias de Rechivaldo, 85

Nájera, 58, 60, 114, 144
Napoleon Route, 1, 20, 149
Navarrete, 58, 59, 65, 128
Niebuhr, Richard R., 1
Nooteboom, Cees, 155n9, 156n19 (chap. 2)

O Cebreiro, 96–100, 102–4, 133, 144,
158nn2–3
Obanos, 48
Orange-Peel Man, the, 24, 28, 86, 124

Palas do Rei, 120
pallozas, 99–100
Pamplona, 25, 26, 30, 38–40, 43, 45, 47,
48, 73, 92, 146

Paris (France), 25, 46, 58, 122, 134, 141,
144
Paul, St., 110–11
Pérez, Antonio, 88
Pérez, Esperanza Nuñez, 100–101,
103–4, 133
Picaud, Aimery, 29–31, 51, 80, 105, 154n2
(chap. 2), 158n6 (chap. 7); *Codex
Calixtinus*, 29, 31, 86, 154n2 (chap. 2),
158n6
pilgrimage, meaning/concept/value of,
3, 6, 11, 13, 15, 35, 47–49, 65, 69, 76, 79,
94, 108–13, 115–16, 118–20, 128, 129,
144–49, 150, 151. *See also* walking
Plato, 109
Población de Campos, 78
Ponferrada, 84, 91, 93, 119
Pope John Paul II, 15
Portela, 97
Portomarín, 116, 120, 128; Fiesta de
Aquardiente, 116
Puente la Reina, 49, 50
Puerta de Ibañeta, 24

Quinn, Anthony, 15

Rabanal del Camino, 86, 87, 89, 90;
Refugio Gaucelmo, 87
Rabé de las Calzadas, 71
Raleigh, Sir Walter, 34
Ras, 122
Red Deer (Alberta), 63, 122
Renche, 107
Reynolds, Neil, 13
Roland, 30, 31, 33; *Chanson de Roland*
(*Song of Roland*), 31
Roncesvalles, 1, 5, 7–9, 17, 18, 20–22, 25,
26, 28, 30, 31, 38, 46, 53, 60, 73, 88, 104,
128–30, 134, 149
Rosario, 120
Rosevear, Anthony and Sherri, 87, 88
Royo, Jésus and Assumpta, 104–6, 108